The Art of Literary Translation

GERMAN LITERATURE, ART & THOUGHT

AN INTERNATIONAL FORUM FOR INTERDISCIPLINARY STUDIES

including THE McMASTER COLLOQUIUM ON GERMAN STUDIES

Edited by **Hans Schulte**

Published by University Press of America
(Lanham, London, New York)

ADVISORY BOARD

The editors will consider any high-quality manuscript, in English or
German, with an interdisciplinary perspective appealing not only to
specialists. Care is taken to ensure a high standard in the quality
and appearance of the volumes. With some pre-formatting and compatible software, production costs will be minimal.

Inquiries, submissions:

Prof. Hans Schulte
McMaster University, Modern Languages
Hamilton, Ontario, Canada L8S 4M2
Tel: (416) 525-9140 ext. 3454 or
FAX: Modern Languages (416) 527-0100

The Art of
LITERARY
TRANSLATION

Edited by

Hans Schulte

&

Gerhart Teuscher

UNIVERSITY
PRESS OF
AMERICA

Lanham • New York • London

Copyright © 1993 by
University Press of America®, Inc.
4720 Boston Way
Lanham, Maryland 20706

3 Henrietta Street
London WC2E 8LU England

Co-published by arrangement with
German Literature Art and Thought, McMaster University

Library of Congress Cataloging-in-Publication Data

The Art of literary translation / edited by Hans Schulte &
Gerhart Teuscher.
p. cm. — (German literature, art & thought)
1. German literature—20th century—Translations into English—
History and criticism. 2. German literature—Translations into
English—History and criticism. 3. Translating and interpreting.
I. Schulte, Hans. II. Teuscher, Gerhart. III. Series.
PT405.A76   1993   418'.02—dc20   92–44343 CIP

ISBN 0–8191–8163–3 (alk. paper)

Table of Contents

Chapter Three — Workshop

Introduction

Art and Critique
The Theory and the Practice of Literary Translation

Hans Schulte
McMaster University

The "Art of Translation. . ." We received this formula, and we repeat it, like an old topos concealing an untruth or a contradiction. We are invited to picture the translator of a literary work side by side with its author, i.e., as a creative writer himself who is engaged, in Goethe's words, in one of the noblest and most significant activities of this world. He (or she, which will be implied from here on) is, after all, an interpreter and at the same time producer of world literature. Without him, our literacy and, indeed, our Western tradition is unthinkable. The translator is that master of language and imagination who re-creates, say, Dante's *Divina Commedia* or Goethe's *Faust* in his own expressive medium. He rises to the author's challenge by compensating for the connotative or evocative text substance lost in the cultural transfer. His receptive and productive powers measure up to the enormity of the task: to bring the world's significant visions of thought and art within the scope of his own cultural community. Without him, this community would be doomed to provincialism.

This ideal image of the literary translator is contradicted, to a striking degree, by his public esteem. Now he appears, all of a sudden, at the bottom of the cultural hierarchy, largely ignored or viewed, with irony, as the literary mechanic who cannot do justice to the literary creator. Accordingly, his publisher pays him a less than modest page fee, which makes him the most notoriously underpaid among all those who earn their living through the written word. Literary translation as an exclusive profession cannot and does not exist. The academic credit of the translator is minimal; in the case of a promotion, a good translation of a novel will count less than a boring, book-length study of its punctuation. It is deemed less "original." The translator normally works in a grey zone; he receives little encouragement and little pertinent criticism from any public or academic source. I exaggerate — though not too much; I wish to make a point.

There are two main causes for this sad state of affairs. First of all, we lost much of the keen sense of inter-cultural sharing and inspiration that once, in the eighteenth and most of the nineteenth century, brought the literary translator to the focus of public attention. And secondly, the quality of translations offered today is in fact all too often unacceptable. Complaining about this has become commonplace. We should rather look into the main causes of the situation, and prepare remedies.

There are three clearly distinguishable groups of writers translating literature: apart from a small group of poets who learn their primary art and craft through the secondary art of translation (more about those later), the market is served by paid translators who cannot take their time (for reasons stated above), and by the dilettantes who have the time but none of the expertise needed (literary, linguistic, cultural knowledge and sensitivity.) The market is open, everyone can enter, no certificates are required. The lack of schooling and of academic and media controls have allowed carelessness and ignorance free rein, considering the basic good faith of the general reader who has no quality control, no access to the language and the literary scope of the original work. The decline of literary translation is even more emphasized by the success, and the qualitative progress, of what we might call the modern translation industry (especially in the areas of business, technology and science.) Here the considerable efforts of translation institutes which are both theory and praxis oriented (the German schools in Heidelberg, Mainz, Saarbrücken, Munich, for example) have paid off handsomely. But even such specialized schools shy away from a systematic integration of literary translation. The explanation often given is that the subject is unteachable. Such an assumption is misleading and, indeed, highly counterproductive, putting its faith in a linguistic-literary instinct, i.e., its natural ability to walk the immensely delicate line of hermeneutic transfer. What we have here is the dangerous claim that the rare exception of genius is the norm. Moreover, this myth invites all kinds of dilettantes to prove that they, indeed, "have it" and should be seen in print.

Fundamentally, literary translation requires considerable, conscious, and teachable knowledge of

1. the principles of intra-lingual and inter-lingual (comparative) semantics and semiotics; the semantics of metaphorical language;
2. translation studies, including the study of approaches according to text types; transfer strategies, including strategies (and limits) of linguistic and literary compensation;
3. hermeneutics of literature and literary translation, both historical and inter-cultural;
4. the cultural, specifically literary histories of both the source and the target languages;
5. comparative literature, incl. critical theory;
6. aesthetics, poetics, stylistics

– not to mention the study and controlled practice of creative writing. Here we have already the outline of a full academic study programme in literary translation, a programme which the neglected craft greatly needs and richly deserves. It might be integrated, at least initially, in the changing and re-selfdefining framework of comparative literature. Or it might find its academic home within the new discipline of translation studies, and move from its periphery more closely to its centre of interests. There are hopeful beginnings, as several of our contributors (Wolfram Wilss, Gerhart Teuscher, Barbara Wright) point out. One of the most dramatically successful mæeutic institutions is the international translation workshop and workplace in Straelen, Germany. Characteristically, however, it arose from a self-help initiative "from outside," i.e., by individual translators, not from inside the academic system. Academic integration, however, even the status that comes with it, would seem essential in view of the plight and social neglect of a profession to which we owe so much of our very literacy and culture.

A comprehensive academic programme such as the one outlined above could achieve that. The graduates would have the choice of becoming professional translators (who would be able, if need be, to present a "critical" translation, with a scholarly apparatus which would permit an optimum of control), or teachers of translation and linguistics, or readers at publishing houses, or critics at major newspapers or magazines. Again, there are beginnings of consistent productivity and quality control in the publishing field, like Leslie Willson's *Dimension* (see his account in this book), however isolated and dependent on some founder's ability and idealism they may be. And there are, increasingly, international symposia like ours inviting poets and their translators, publishers, literary scholars and translation scholars to enter into a constructive dialogue, and to further critical insight and expertise as well as public awareness of the vital art of literary translation.

*

Criticism, I suggest, is of greatest importance in this potentially treacherous field of cultural production. The resolutely "practical" translator, who refuses to be paralyzed by the pale cast of academic thought, is usually paralyzed by prejudice. Here are a few of his questionable sentiments (always assuming that, as is normally the case, his target language and his mother tongue are one and the same:)

1) *I must make sure that I translate into a smooth modern idiom.* This is one of the most dangerous misconceptions. "Smoothness" usually implies what Nietzsche called "das Durchschnittliche, Mittlere, Mitteilsame," i.e., the "vulgarizing" spirit of language, in this case of the target language – not the author's unique and provocative linguistic vision. In fact, such a precept ignores a twofold challenge: 1) the author's work against the grain of his own language system, and 2) centennia of another culture stored in the source system, to court and challenge the target system. The translator of literature is not asked to familiarize, i.e., to force the original design into the narrow and shallow confines of colloquialism, but to alienate the consumer, i.e., to accommodate that forceful design, within the "stubborn" referential system of the target language, through bold associations, contextual shifts of meaning, and even a certain daring literalism that would reclaim, as it were, semantic territory lost in the transfer. Every common language wants to enslave. If we succumb as users to this lure of commonness, we lose our individuality; if we do so as translators of literature, we also declare bankruptcy as productive agents of world culture. The god that inspires is always "other." Every true artist knows it. The true translator knows it, too, since his is the inspiration which turns a craft into an art. Creative alienation, therefore, is one of the fundamental principles of literary translation. Hölderlin – to cite an extreme example – religiously shielded his vision of Greek antiquity, in his rendition of *Antigone*, from the onslaught of linguistic vulgarity in his own time and culture. In the process he stretched the capacity of the German language to the point of cruelty and violation. His translation was often called private and esoteric. Brecht, however, the master of down-to-earth dialogue, praised the alienating productivity of that half-forgotten translation very highly, and based his own adaptation on it.

Germany has long been the classical country of translation and its theory, especially through the so-called *Goethezeit*. We should not forget that the "otherness" of Greek, Roman, English, French, Italian, Spanish, and Eastern literatures converging on the German cultural scene represents a powerful factor in the country's literary renewal. Virtually all influential translations, especially the "classical" ones, betray that provocative strangeness, and most theories (from Herder's to Goethe's, Humboldt's and the Romantics') defend it. Today we seem to have lost such self-denying openness; the overpowering syncretism of modern economy, science, and technology, the rationalism of intra-lingual and inter-lingual communication systems is largely responsible for this loss.

2) *A good translator is the servant of his author. His function is to reconstruct the author's intentions in another linguistic medium.* This is the reverse of 1), and equally misleading. We are dealing with the typical submissive gesture of the positivistic historians of the nineteenth century, the inter-lingual (inter-cultural) equivalent, in fact, of historicism. But whereas historicism has long become a fact of history itself, its inter-lingual counterpart is – due largely to a lack of scholarship and hermeneutic criticism in the field of translation – still very much alive. We need to be reminded that *Wirkungsgeschichte*, to use Hans-Georg Gadamer's term, is a fundamental category of both the interpretation of texts from another time and from another language; interpretation and translation become identical concepts in both directions. The Romantics, as we all know, were the first to discover this phenomenon. Their message is still valid today: the translator's function and goal is the "progression" of "universal poetry" (Novalis), not its regression to a *status quo*.

The translator's task is not simply the "transfer" of a poet's text to another medium, but the establishment of a new literary *paradigm*. Michael Hamburger arguably created the English paradigm of Paul Celan, just like a consensus of eighteenth century readers and critics created a German paradigm of *Hamlet*. Such "readers and critics" are, in fact, translators, but only in one predominant sense. For criticism is also a collective, flexible enterprise; its paradigms are unfixed sums. Translation, however, is focused and fixed, a literary creation itself, i.e., a fundamental text which generates its own tradition of readers and critics. The translator is at first his author's interpreter; but in the course of the social production process he virtually becomes his co-author. The burden of this responsibility is, indeed, extraordinary.

But quite apart from the hermeneutic problem, a translator's submissive, all-too faithful attitude is clearly unproductive. It basically provides two options: literalism and wordiness. Literalism, as mentioned above and demonstrated impressively by George Steiner, can indeed be a high art in the hands of a master. Hölderlin's and Schleiermacher's translations from the Greek are classical examples. But the magic will turn to loss and destruction in the hands of a servant. Words, and especially the words a poet turns to, are infinitely connotative; to him, this aura is more essential to the texture of his work than the conceptual content. A word (like Hofmannsthal's "Abend") may carry or even constitute an entire poem, as a magical conjuration deeply rooted in the memory of the speaker and his culture. The very sound of the word is an integral part of its impact. An equivalent does not exist, and even a good contextual motivation rarely pulls the foreign focus within reach. What usually happens in a "submissive" translation is an unacceptable loss of complexity and mystery, and of the structural, musical and semantic interplay within the work that constitutes its "meaning."

Quite often the frustrated translator, who finds a gap in the matrix of his target language where he had groped for some equivalent, resorts to filling this gap with descriptive material; he then forgets the fundamental fact that literary texts and each of their elements *mean* and *are* at the same time, and that depriving them of their "being" (through wordy rationalizations) is really synonymous with depriving them of their literariness. This tendency to "fill the gaps" with busy words accounts for the fact that so many translations of literature are considerably longer than their originals. We are tempted to build a coherent facade with the building behind it missing. We forget that the work itself is never a "com-

plete report," and that its own words are posted around the inex-
pressible, i.e., around silence. This is particularly true of the literature (and especially poetry) of our time which, for this very reason,
presents a tremendous challenge to the evocative powers of the
translator.

I realize that my analysis of error seems to resurrect the old
truism of the "impossiblity" and "treachery" of translation. Nothing could be further from my intention. We simply should be aware
of the pitfalls where we carry the "truth" of literature across the
borders of languages. If we are, and if we are free from the vices of
complacency or submissiveness, we can even turn the supposedly
inevitable loss into a gain. All that is required is an active sharing,
not just an understanding, of the author's primary vision and
design; a confident knowledge that the original text is, within the
confines of its language, never complete but part of a process,
charged with potential. A new language and life must be given to
this potential and as much semantic territory as possible provided
at the same time for the complex "otherness" of the present work.
The author passes the baton: now it is his, the translator's race – a
race with the challenge and chance to do even better. And a good
part of this chance is the target language and culture which could
unleash, within the work's "potential," forces and dimensions of
meaning which the author's own medium had denied him.

3) *Translation is to rise above the two language systems. I am the man
in the middle, retrieving shared thought and feeling.* The "mythic"
hypostases of source and target texts are followed by a third falla-
cious theorem, i.e., the universalist position of mediation. The concept "middle" is indeed, as an ideal construct, useless and misleading in practical terms. The prospect of transcending Babel has never
ceased to fascinate writers and thinkers, from the mystics to the
rationalists, materialists and biologists, incl. Marxism and the mental "deep structures" of Noam Chomsky. Walter Benjamin, an especially impressive case, returns to the mystic tradition. In translating, he claims, we follow an erotic urge to re-unite; ideally, the
translator stands, between the languages, on a piece of pre-Babel

paradise. We feel reminded of pre-Romantic, gnostic-inspired philosophies of "love" and "sympathy" in the eighteenth century: since we are all scattered fragments of divinity, a progressive, universal re-union will ultimately re-produce God. Ancient spiritualism seems to conspire with modern science and commerce to undo Babel, and to devise a theory and strategy which would prove destructive to the translator of literature. There is a primacy of self-expression and individual culture (which includes group culture) in languages – an insight which George Steiner has most eloquently, if ineffectually, argued. Steiner reaffirmed the individualist tradition of philosophical linguistics, which dates back to Herder and Humboldt, – a highly unpopular choice in the age of multi-national corporations. *Ideologiekritik* of Steiner's work has become commonplace in linguistic and translation research, especially in North America. Contemporary translation studies have returned to a rational universalism – "cognition" is now the key concept. A linguistic theory, however, which serves the interests of world economy, world politics, and even world peace, does not necessarily serve the interest of art. It is a commonplace insight that linguistic generalization goes against the grain of linguistic productivity. The more collective and ultimately intercultural linguistic concepts become, the more thinned out, uprooted and even dehumanized they will be. This is the secondary, collective tendency of language that Humboldt talked about: to estrange man from himself and nature ("Gewalt gegen den Menschen auszuüben"); in this age of internationalism, the primary inward drive of language, the source of its creative power, is discredited, disclaimed, and "deconstructed."

Both poets and translators are called upon to "heal" our language; German authors towards the end of the eighteenth century dramatically regenerated their language out of its own latent powers (or "heart,") and in militant opposition to the rational, universalist tendencies of the age. This led, as we all know, to an unparalleled upsurge of literary culture. Today such a retrieval seems even more urgent. The conscientious poet and translator of this

century suffers the crisis of Hofmannsthal's Lord Chandos in per-
manence: the pent-up complexity of the vision, and the ineptness
and banality of a current sign system which cannot support it.
Which tells us that in becoming more needed than ever, the arts of
literature and of translation have also become so much more difficult, even though the history of rhetoric and poetics shows that the
conviction *semper mens est potentior quam sint verba* was strong,
indeed, at all times. But if we accept this statement, are we not, as
critics of universalist linguistics, unwittingly relapsing into a mys-
tic-absolutist frame of mind? Would we not expect a truer antithesis
to semantic universalism, i.e., the concept of autonomous sign
systems determining their contents of thought? Many excellent
arguments, indeed, speak for this radical view – which would be
potentially disastrous to the translator. The poets themselves have
frequently contributed to the semantic shifts that changed our
perception of being. "Es rauschten leis die Wälder" Eichendorff
sang and enriched the word "Wald" and the cultural self-understanding of its users in a highly idiosyncratic way. Language
founds and characterizes nations – Willa Muir once went as far as
to relate Hitler's Third Reich to the "purposive control" and "clot-
ted abstractions" of the German sentence structure. Language di-
rects our intellect and even our sense perceptions: a German ear
really *hears* a pig utter "ruff ruff", as its language asserts, and not
"oink oink" which is the English "equivalent." Perception, thought,
speech, writing are understood, by linguists and philosophers, as
making selections within the complex sets of meanings called languages. There is no meaning outside language, and – in Wittgenstein's terms – "you don't know what you mean before you can say
it." But the poet as well as his congenial translator knows that this
is only a half-truth. They will never re-produce a current "bour-
geois" system of meaning if not to expose, to criticize, to parody.
Goethe in his "Werther" suggested two attitudes towards language. Albert, safe in his middle-class fortress of verbal judgements
and moral antitheses, sees no reason to question a language that
thinks for him, moralizes for him, and provides him with high

standing and office. Werther, unadjusted and unsafe socially and politically, makes language the expressive instrument of his infinite, dynamic vision and longing, repeatedly driving it to the limit of its capacity. Albert lives, a social success, and Werther must die. Yet Werther will live, posthumously, forever, since his word alone remains memorable, moving, and inspiring.

*

In recent years we have heard new and increasing support for literal translation once advocated by idealist poets and philosophers, but for new and almost diametrically opposite reasons. While idealist literalism, like Hölderlin's, was to protect the poem's *sanctum* ("das Heilige") against destruction by the idioms of other times and language cultures, this post-modern literalism is freely employed as an alienation device to expose this "Heilige" as pseudo-truth, and to provide a text for a critical modern discourse. For the translator's function and self-understanding, this new *ethos* is, indeed, nothing short of revolutionary, if potentially catastrophic. It is also undeniably seductive, since he, the translator, is now finally on an equal footing with the author (a term which – if admissible at all – no longer signifies an "original" writer's privilege.) He even ranks higher in the enlightened pyramid; while traditionally the author was deemed free and the translator was bound and subservient, the reverse is now believed to be the case: the "author" is bound to his *mythos*, while the translator is critically free. Any commitment to textual authority, including the author's "meaning," is cancelled. The monument of "the work" has to fall, so that "a text" may be available to future literary discourse.

It seems to me, however, that a translation theory combatting the very idea of culture will not succeed in motivating the hard work of linguistic transfer. Lively intellectual exchange activities between nations are based on one fundamental expectation, i.e., the mutual gift and reception of culture. And part of this expectation is the old understanding that any significant work of national culture implies an *Erkenntnis* (if I may use a German term which is less burdened metaphysically than "truth.") Without it, any intellectual consensus, and any collective orientation and interest will be lost. A translation deconstructing *Faust* or, say, the Bible, will hardly be a popular success. It can be safely said that *Ideologiekritik*, of Marxist or post-structuralist provenance, has not yet proven its usefulness as a productive tool in the hands of the translator.

Recently I came across a volume of proceedings from a Musil symposium in Straelen. Sure enough, there was more than one contribution promoting deconstructionist translation theory. But the vast majority of papers were of a much more traditional nature: all intellectual and intuitive powers were employed to provide the safest possible transfer to the author's inviolable word.

Both attitudes, i.e., mythical reverence and parodic irreverence towards the author and his work, are problematic. A more constructive principle may be found somewhere between these extremes. I would like to give you an interesting example. Hans Magnus Enzensberger was a keynote speaker at the original symposium behind this volume. His topic: "The Sinking of the Titanic: The Poet as his own Translator." Enzensberger admitted in his talk that he had not been interested primarily, as a translator of his own work, in making it known to the English-speaking public. His interest was in the creative learning experience concerning his own original text, his production methods, cultural prejudice, problems with the German language etc. Approaching his own work from the other culture and language system allowed him to break up his product, expose its relative one-sidedness, and the specificity of a culture at its base. The author as translator had not sworn an oath of allegiance to himself, and was therefore free to act as a radical critic of his text.

So far went the "deconstruction" of Enzensberger's model. However, the whole purpose of the author-translator was to demolish in order to re-construct. The translator Enzensberger saw himself in the role of an art restorer: the picture was to be rejuvenated, regenerated, cleansed, retouched. The primary experience, the message or "Erkenntnis" emanating from a cultural-linguistic community, was never really threatened through this radical process. On the contrary, it was deepened, freed from confining structural circumstances, and from secondary cultural and linguistic blocks and biases. Enzensberger offered this model for a revised self-understanding of the translator. It is based on the assumption that there can be an even closer symbiosis between author/work and translator than before. The model implies an unprecedented critical and creative liberation, but it also presupposes a profound insight in the author's hidden design. The analogy of the art restorer is, of course, slightly misleading: the original picture is or at least was "there," and restoration is reconstruction. The literary author's "original," however, is much more hypothetical. In fact, the author Hans Magnus Enzensberger needed to translate his text to bring it into the open. There are great difficulties, of course, implied in this proposed new standard of excellence in translation, but they are far outweighed by its productive potential. Enzensberger's model is in many ways compatible with certain non-Western attitudes towards translation. In China and Japan, my colleague Koichi Shinohara explains, no pressures of national states have led to myths and mystifications of "individual" culture, and notions like the "externality" and "untranslatibility" of texts are unheard-of. Western texts read in the light of Japanese culture and *vice versa* are considered intellectual activities of the highest order, and of enormous productive and corrective potential. As in Enzensberger's case, the translatability of a text is the true test of its relevance. No longer the "traitor" (Croce's *traduttore–traditore*) of a relatively modern European convention, the translator is implicitly given the status of international co-author. His free-and-critical intercultural practice, I would suggest, can indeed achieve what is needed most in any future history of the human spirit: the internalization of "individual" works of national culture into a world culture.

*

The contributions in this volume originated, as mentioned, from a symposium at McMaster university. They are no conventional "proceedings," however, but were re-worked, expanded and updated where necessary, and in two cases (Hans-Georg Gadamer's and my own contribution) newly written for this book. The difficulties on its way to publication appeared, at one point, insurmountable, but could finally, with the help of a new publisher, be resolved. I owe a special debt of gratitude to Gerhart Teuscher, my untiring co-editor. We both wish to thank the contributors for their patience and good faith.

Chapter One

Principles

Lesen ist Übersetzen

Hans-Georg Gadamer
Heidelberg, Germany

Ein berühmtes Wort von Benedetto Croce sagt: "traduttore-tra-ditore". Jede Übersetzung ist wie ein Verrat. Wie sollte das der Mann nicht wissen, der so polyglott war, wie der bedeutende italienische Ästhetiker – oder wie jemand wie ich, der als Hermeneutiker sein lebenlang auf die Nebentöne, die Ober- und Untertöne von Sprache zu achten gelernt hat. Obendrein muß ich gestehen: man wird mit den Jahren immer empfindlicher gegen die Viertel- und Halb-Annäherungen an wirklich lebendige Sprache, die als Übersetzungen begegnen. Man findet sie immer schwerer zu ertragen und obendrein immer schwerer zu verstehen.

Jedenfalls ist es ein hermeneutisches Thema, über Grade nicht der Übersetzbarkeit, sondern der Unübersetzbarkeit nachzudenken – über das, was verloren geht, wo übersetzt wird, und vielleicht auch, was dabei gewonnen wird. Selbst bei diesem hoffnungslos scheinenden Verlustgeschäft des Übersetzens gibt es nicht nur ein Mehr oder Weniger an Verlust, es gibt auch mitunter so etwas wie Gewinn, mindestens einen Interpretationsgewinn, einen Zuwachs an Deutlichkeit und Eindeutigkeit.

Sprachliches, das als Text begegnet, und das heißt, was dem ursprünglichen Gesprächsleben, in dem Sprache leibt und lebt, schon entfremdet ist, ist selten von so vollendeter Genauigkeit, daß stets das rechte Wort gewählt und gefunden ist. Viel verlegenes Darumherumreden, viel Ausflucht in die Leerformeln trivialer

Rhetorik schiebt sich ein, und wenn es sich um Übersetzungen handelt, geschieht das gleich zweimal: einmal beim schreibenden Autor, der in leere Konvention abgleitet, ein andermal beim schreibenden Übersetzer, dem das gleiche droht. Das macht die 'Nachricht' des Textes ungenau. Ja, es ist geradezu für den Autor wie eine Erziehung zur Klarheit und Knappheit des Ausdrucks, wenn er etwa als Deutscher vom Englischen Gebrauch macht oder auch nur – als gebranntes Kind, das das Feuer scheut – für einen Übersetzer schreibt, und das heißt, im Blick auf den Leser der kommenden Übersetzung. Da wird man den langen Perioden aus dem Wege gehen, die wir so lieben und die uns durch die humanistische Bewunderung Ciceros anerzogen sind, und den seelenvollen Dunkelheiten auch, in die es uns lockt.

Die Kunst des Schreibens zielt am Ende immer darauf, wie die der lebendigen Rede, den anderen "zum Verstehen zu zwingen" (um mit Fichte zu reden). Nichts von dem, was die Mittel der lebendigen Rede gewähren, ist dabei dem Schreibenden vergönnt. Wenn es sich nicht gerade um einen Privatbrief handelt, kennt der Schreibende seinen Leser nicht. Er kann nicht spüren, wo der andere nicht mitgeht, er kann also auch nicht nachstoßen, wo es an der rechten Überzeugungskraft fehlte. Dazu kommt: Was der Schreiber an Überzeugungskraft aufbringt, muß er allein durch die starren Zeichen der Schrift erreichen. Die Artikulation, die Modulation, die Rhythmisierung der Rede, laut und leise, Nachdruck und leichte Anspielung – und, was das stärkste Mittel aller überzeugenden Rede ist, das Zögern, die Pause, das Suchen und das Finden des Wortes, so daß es wie ein Glücksfund ist, an dem der Zuhörer mit fast freudigem Erschrecken teilhat – all das soll durch nichts als niedergeschriebene Zeichen ersetzt werden. Dabei ist es oft ein Schreiber, der gar kein Schriftsteller ist, kein Könner und Künstler des Schreibens, sondern irgend ein Gelehrter oder Wissenschaftler, ein Forscher, der sich ins Unbekannte gewagt hat und nun erzählen soll, wie es da aussieht und wie es da zugeht.

Was wird da alles vom Übersetzer verlangt! Man möchte ein witziges Wort auf ihn anwenden, das Friedrich Schlegel einmal von dem verstehenden Leser, dem Interpreten, gesagt hat: "Um jemanden zu verstehen, muß man erstlich klüger sein als er, dann ebenso klug und dann auch ebenso dumm. Es ist nicht genug, daß man den eigentlichen Sinn eines konfusen Werkes besser versteht, als der Autor es verstanden hat. Man muß auch die Konfusion selbst bis auf die Prinzipien kennen, charakterisieren und konstruieren können." Das Letztere ist das allerschwerste. Man riskiert, noch dümmer zu sein als der andere, wenn man aus dem eigenen weiteren Umblick und der klareren Einsicht die Meinung des gelesenen Textes überzeugend zum Sprechen bringen will.

Übersetzte Texte zu lesen ist im allgemeinen schwer. Es fehlt der Atem des Sprechenden, es fehlt das Volumen der Sprache. Gleichwohl sind Übersetzungen manchmal für den Kenner des Originals echte Verständnishilfen. Übersetzungen von griechischen oder lateinischen Schriftstellern ins Französische oder von deutschen Schriftstellern ins Englische sind oft von verblüffender und erhellender Eindeutigkeit. Das ist doch wohl ein Gewinn. Oder?

Wo es um nichts als Erkenntnis geht, oder auch nur um nichts als die Erfassung des in einem Text Gemeinten, mag das wohl ein Gewinn sein –– so wie etwa die Photographie einer nur schwer sichtbaren Skulptur in einem düsteren Dom Gewinn bringt. Oder es mag bei manchem Buch der Forschung oder der Lehre ganz und gar nicht auf die Kunst des Schreibens ankommen und damit vielleicht auch gar nicht auf die Kunst des Übersetzens, sondern auf richtige Information. Fachleute verstehen einander (wenn sie wollen) sehr leicht, und gewiß verdrießt es sie eher, wenn man zu viele schöne Worte macht, so wie es einen bei mündlicher Mitteilung verdrießt, wenn einer weiter ausführen will, was man schon längst verstanden hat. Eine Anekdote mag die Sache verdeutlichen: Von dem jungen Karl Jaspers wird erzählt, daß er eines Tages, als er mit einem Kollegen über sein erstes Buch sprach und von diesem zu hören bekam, es sei schlecht geschrieben, geantwortet habe: "Sie hätten mir nichts Angenehmeres sagen können" – so sehr folgte Jaspers damals dem Sachlichkeitspathos seines großen Vorbildes Max Weber. Der zum Denker von eigener Statur gereifte

Karl Jaspers freilich schrieb dann selber einen so kunstvollen und individuellen Stil, daß er kaum übersetzbar ist.

Ja, 'Grade der Unübersetzbarkeit'! Man kann es begreifen, daß in vielen Wissenschaften das Englische sich mehr und mehr durchsetzt, so daß die Forscher ihre Originalarbeiten gleich auf Englisch schreiben. Da sind sie freilich nicht nur vor ihren eigenen 'schönen Worten' sicher, sondern auch vor dem Übersetzer. Längst schon ist das Englische in vielen Bereichen, z.b. in Schiffahrt, Luftfahrt und Nachrichtentechnik, in einem sicheren Jenseits von Gut und Böse der Übersetzerkunst standardisiert. Kein Zufall: Dort kommt es auf richtiges Verstehen wirklich an. Dort ist es lebensgefährlich, mißzuverstehen.

Aber es gibt die Literatur. Da ist nichts gefährlich. Da ist aber auch ein solcher Ausweg versperrt. Da schreibt man für die Menschen gleicher Zunge, und die gemeinsame Muttersprache trägt einen. Es muß nicht nur die 'schöne' Literatur im vollen Sinne des Wortes sein. Es fragt sich doch wirklich (gegen den jungen Jaspers), ob es für einen Historiker oder Philologen und selbst beim Philosophen (wo man streiten mag) ein wirklicher Vorzug ist, 'schlecht' zu schreiben. Erst recht gilt das von Übersetzungen. In Wahrheit ist der 'Stil' mehr als eine entbehrliche oder gar verdächtige Dekoration. Er ist vielmehr ein Faktor, der die Lesbarkeit ausmacht – und damit auch für die Übersetzung eine eigene Aufgabe darstellt. Es ist das keine Sache handwerklicher Technik allein. Eine lesbare Übersetzung ist, wenn sie auch noch einigermaßen 'zuverlässig' ist, schon viel, ja beinahe alles, was man sich als Autor oder Übersetzer – oder als Leser – wünschen kann.

Aber wenn es sich wirklich um 'Literatur' handelt, kann dieser Maßstab nicht mehr genügen. Die Grade der Unübersetzbarkeit richten sich drohend auf, wie ein vielschichtiges Riesengebirge, als dessen letzter Höhenzug die lyrische Poesie aufragt, vom ewigen Schnee verklärt. Damit differenzieren sich natürlich die Ansprüche und die Maßstäbe für das Gelingen von Übersetzung. Nehmen wir zum Beispiel zur Reproduktion bestimmte Übersetzungen, wie es das heute für Theaterstücke gibt. Da soll die Übersetzung nicht nur lesbar, sondern auch sprechbar und bühnengerecht sein, ob in Prosa oder in Versen. Von Gundolfs mit Georges Beistand dichterisch vollendeter Übersetzung Shakespeares, die fast schon eine Eindeutschung heißen muß, sagt man, daß sie nicht spielbar sei. Mancher mag sie heute nicht einmal lesbar finden.

Aber wenn wir überhaupt an Verse denken, sind wir schon mitten in einer höchst diffizilen Problematik. Da ist kaum noch Einigkeit über die Zielvorstellung einer Übersetzung zu erwarten. Ist das Ziel Worttreue oder Sinn- und Form-Treue? Doch gilt das fast ebenso schon von jeder künstlerischen Prosa. Was ist da das Ziel? Wenn man an die große Übersetzungsliteratur denkt, die etwa den englischen Roman nach Deutschland brachte, oder an die Übersetzungen der großen russischen Romane in die anderen Weltsprachen, sieht man sogleich, daß der Verlust an Eigenem, an Volksnähe, an Kraft und Saft, der unvermeidlicherweise dabei eintritt, kaum ins Gewicht fällt gegenüber der Präsenz dessen, was da erzählt wird. Wie es erzählt wird, das ist nicht so sehr Kunst des Wortes. Da kommt es auf anderes an, auf Anschaulichkeit, auf Spannungsdichte, auf Seelentiefe, auf Weltzauber. Die Kunst des Erzählens ist ein eigenes Wunder, das selbst in Übersetzungen ungeschmälert bleibt. Kenner des Russischen versichern einem, daß die deutsche Dostojewski-Übersetzung der Piper-Ausgabe (von Rhasin) dem stockenden, holprigen, forcierten Stil Dostojewskis durch ihre Glätte und Lesbarkeit wenig angemessen ist – und doch, wenn man Nötzels oder Eliasbergs 'bessere' Übersetzung stattdessen nimmt oder die neuesten, im Aufbau-Verlag herausgekommenen: man merkt als Leser die Unterschiede überhaupt nicht. Die Schranke des Unübersetzbaren ist hier – von Sonderfällen wie dem von Gogol abgesehen – außerordentlich niedrig.

Es ist wohl kein Zufall, daß die Prägung des Begriffs der Weltliteratur, die von Übersetzungen unabtrennbar ist, mit der Ausbreitung der Romankunst und der dramatischen Leseliteratur gleichzeitig war. Es ist die Ausbreitung der Lesekultur, die die Literatur zur Literatur gemacht hat. So muß man fast sagen: Literatur ist Übersetzungsliteratur, eben weil sie Lesekultur ist. Tatsächlich ist das Geheimnis des Lesens wie eine große Brücke zwischen den Sprachen. Auf ganz verschiedenen Niveaus scheint es die gleiche hermeneutische Leistung. Schon das Lesen von Texten in der eigenen Muttersprache ist ja wie eine Übersetzung, fast wie eine Übersetzung in eine Fremdsprache, Umsetzung in ein neues Medium, das der Klänge und des Flusses der Rede. Es ist nicht nur Verstehen, sondern Auslegung – beim bloßen Lesen originaler oder übersetzter Texte Auslegung, die in Ton und Tempo liegt, in Modulation und Artikulation der 'inneren Stimme' für das 'innere Ohr', beim tatsächlichen Übersetzen aus einer fremden Sprache überdies Auslegung in ein neues Text-Ganzes aus Sinn und Klang. Beides verlangt eine ans Schöpferische grenzende Umsetzung.

Man kann das Paradox wagen: jeder Leser ist wie ein Übersetzer. Ist es nicht wahrlich am Ende das größere Wunder, daß man den Abstand zwischen Lettern und lebendiger Rede zu überwinden vermag, als daß man den Abstand zwischen zwei Sprachen im lebendigen Verständigungsversuch überspielt? Ist es nicht jedenfalls das Lesen, das die eine Entfernung wie die andere, die zwischen Text und Rede und die zwischen verschiedenen Sprachen, am ehesten überwindet? Lesen ist wie ein Über-setzen von einem Ufer zu einem fernen anderen, und ebenso ist das Tun des Übersetzers eines 'Textes' Über-setzen von Küste zu Küste, von einem Festland zum anderen, von Text zu Text. Übersetzen ist beides. Die Lautgestalten verschiedener Zungen dagegen sind unübersetzbar. Sie scheinen wie durch Sternenjahre voneinander entfernt.

Und in der Tat, da ist das Gedicht, das man nicht nur lesen soll, sondern hören muß. Hier sind die Übersetzer mit ihrem Latein am Ende. Oder besser: Was sie vorlegen, bleibt Latein. Gewiß, es gibt Sonderfälle. Wenn ein wirklicher Dichter die Verse eines anderen Dichters in seine eigene Sprache überträgt, mag das ein wirkliches Gedicht werden. Aber dann ist es fast mehr sein eigenes Gedicht als das des ursprünglichen Autors. Georges Baudelaire-Übersetzungen, sind sie überhaupt noch 'Blumen des Bösen'? Schallen sie nicht eher wie Vorklänge einer neuen Jugend? Es ist, als ob der Dichter, der hier am Werke ist, dem unerhörten Sinnenzauber des

Moralisten den hellen Seelenton einer strahlenden Gesundheit entlockt hätte. Oder Rilkes Valéry-Übersetzungen: wo bleibt da das scharfe Licht und die Härte der Provence, in diesen wunderbar weichen Meditationen über den 'Friedhof am Meer'? Wir tun wahrlich gut, so etwas Nachdichtungen zu nennen.

Dagegen kann ein Übersetzer, der kein Dichter ist, keinen eigenen Ton anschlagen und durchhalten. Seinen eigenen Ton kann man nicht wählen. Er ist für den wirklichen Dichter seine zweite Natur. Die Folge ist: wenn ein Übersetzer, der kein Dichter ist, in seiner eigenen Sprache poetische Äquivalente zur fremden Sprache zusammenzufügen genötigt ist, dann klingt es am Ende immer wie "Lateinisch", das heißt, künstlich und fremd. Da mögen noch so viele poetische Anklänge an Gutes und Schönes aus der Literatur der Zielsprache dazwischentönen, es fehlt der Ton, der 'tonos', die gespannte Saite, die unter den Worten und Tönen beben muß, wenn Gesang sein soll. Wie sollte es auch anders sein.

Äquivalente müßten nicht nur für die Wortbedeutungen gefunden werden, sondern ebenso auch für die Klänge. Aber nein, weder Worte, noch so ansprechende, noch auch Klänge, noch so ansprechende, genügen dafür. Verse sind Sätze. Aber nein, nicht einmal das ist es: es sind Verse, und das ganze ist ein Gedicht, ein Gesang, eine Melodie (es muß nicht einmal eine Melodie sein, die sich wiederholt). Stets wird es ein Widerklang sein, ein Sinnklang aus Einem und Vielem, wie die verborgene Harmonie, die stärker ist als die offene, wie Heraklit gewußt hat.

So sollten wir alle Übersetzer bewundern, die uns den Abstand zum Original nicht verbergen und ihn doch zugleich überbrücken. Sie sind Interpreten. Das heißt, sie reden dazwischen, wie wir Ausleger es ohnehin tun. Aber sie sind mehr. Unser, der Ausleger, größter Ehrgeiz kann es nur sein, daß unsere Interpretation ins Lesen der originalen Texte wie selbstverständlich eingeht und darin verschwindet. Dagegen bleibt des Übersetzers Text mitdichtende Spur für unser aller Lesen und Verstehen. Ein eigener fester Bestand aus Sinn und Klang. Sein Text ist wie eine Brücke, die von beiden Seiten begehbar ist, eine Brücke zwischen zwei Ufern in einem einzigen Land. Über solche Brücken geht ein beständig fließender Verkehr. Das macht des Übersetzens Auszeichnung aus. Wir Interpreten bleiben einsame Spaziergänger, die sich hin und wieder einmal mit einem Leser treffen.

Translation Studies

The State of the Art

Wolfram Wilss
Universität des Saarlandes

According to the theoretical principles of modern research, most persuasively formulated by the philosophy of science (Wissenschaftstheorie), it is the task of a specific branch of a science (Einzelwissenschaft) to describe and explain the respective topic and, in doing so, to develop an adequate methodology. The object of translation studies (TS) can be circumscribed as consisting of three areas of research:

1. the source language (SL) text analysis,

2. the interlingual transfer (in the narrower sense of the word) - going from SL text to target language (TL) text,

3. the TL translation result.

As a consequence, the task of TS is, in basic terms, twofold:

1. It must develop plausible methods for a translation-oriented text analysis, for the description and explanation of interlingual transfer procedures, and for the description and explanation of the transfer result.

2. It must lay down adequate criteria for the formation of an objective frame of reference covering both the prospective, process-oriented and the retrospective, result-oriented dimension of translation.

Now, this is more easily said than done, and it is obvious that TS

– and this applies to an even higher degree to machine translation (MT) – has raised problems rather than provided satisfactory answers and solutions. This is due to the fact that translation, apart from interlingual standard phraseology, e.g. in phatic communication, is a highly involved area of language usage (Newmark, 1988).

The structural complexity of interlingual transfer procedures becomes abundantly clear in the following three transfer definitions:

1. Translating is a cognitive activity (Krings, 1986) in the course of which the translator, by carrying out a sequence of text-bound code-switching operations, reproduces an SL message in a TL, thus making this message, ideally in all its semantic, functional and pragmatic dimensions, accessible to a TL reader. In other words: the translator, as the recipient of the SL message, analyses the message to be translated with the help of his linguistic, extralinguistic and sociocultural text knowledge, and in a second step, as the TL sender, performs the interlingual transfer (Nida/Reyburn, 1981). In doing this, he uses TL signs, sign combinations and sign-combination rules which he selects from the TL repertoire in accordance with his aim of achieving semantic and stylistic translation equivalence (Nida/Taber, 1969). In principle every translation is characterized, admittedly to a lesser or higher degree, as the case may be, by the personal finger-print of the translator (Wilss, 1988a). As we shall see later on this is, above all, true in the field of literary translation. Just as two finger-prints are never a hundred percent alike, there are no fully identical TL versions in the event of multiple translation of the same text by different translators, even if they possess a comparable level of translation competence. The only case of total text identity as the result of the transfer of one and the same text by several translators under comparable transfer conditions is the so-called Septuagint. This achievement is, however, a legend carefully preserved by the Church especially in the Middle Ages. This legend is motivated by the sacrosanct character of the Holy Scriptures which led Jerome to make a consistent distinction, in terms of transfer methods, between the transfer of

biblical and secular texts. The efficiency of the translator's transfer strategy depends on his transfer competence which can be factorized on a semiotic basis. All competence levels, the syntactic, the semantic and the pragmatic level, must be correlated and integrated functionally; the ability to correlate and integrate the various layers of a text is a prerequisite for the translator to conduct the interlingual transfer under semasiological and onomasiological aspects and thus to bring about a translation result with an optimum degree of intertextual equivalence.

2. Translating is a sequence of code-switching operations leading from a written SL text to an optimally equivalent written TL text and requires the linguistic and extralinguistic comprehension of the SL text by the translator in his role as SL text recipient. Communicatively speaking, a text simply does not exist without a reader. This is true of both monolingual and interlingual communication. "Of course no one denies the existence of a text as ink on paper even without an experiencer, but there seem to be qualities beyond that which could be claimed do not exist if the text is not read" (Cassirer, 1978, 3). Text understanding, no matter if in a monolingual or in a translational context, is partly of an objective, partly of a subjective nature. "Wenn sich die Qualität eines Textes durch das Bedeutungspotential bestimmt, das ein Leser in dessen Angebot zu finden vermag, so ist sie sowohl von textuellen Gegebenheiten wie von der Lesebefähigung des Rezipienten abhängig" (Fritsch, 1981,-631). It is evident that the influence of the translator on the translation result is more noticeable in cases where he must, in order to achieve an acceptable translation result, invest a lot of cognitive and stylistic skills than in cases where he can fall back upon linguistically and referentially standardized texts which reduce his stylistic leeway to a bare minimum or even to zero and permit only obligatory syntactic and semantic shifts of expression (Wilss, 1981a). This is particularly the case in language for special purposes (LSP) texts which confront the translator with the task of retaining, above all, equivalence on the content level: The universally logical function of LSP texts guarantees, provided the respective com-

municative partners possess a comparable level of linguistic and extralinguistic knowledge (world knowledge), optimal communicative conditions and, as a rule, an optimal degree of translatability. The denotational frame of reference of LSP texts eliminates, as it were, the text sender and the text recipient as subjective factors of LSP text production and text reception. As a result of widespread surface standardization, LSP communication is an excellent example of an ideal sender/recipient relation in the Chomsky-propagated sense of the word. If anywhere at all, it is in the realm of LSP texts that one can venture to speak of model translation. This does, however, not permit the conclusion that, in the last analysis, it is possible to reduce transfer procedures in LSP texts to standardized equivalence relations and, in consequence, to predict, in a reliable fashion, all transfer operations and to pre-assess the degree of translation equivalence obtainable in each particular case. Anyone arguing along such lines would be in danger of overestimating textual and translational typification trends and, at the same time, of underestimating the inherent surface complexity and diversity so characteristic of concrete text occurrences even in the realm of LSP texts. Strictly speaking, full typification and regularization of texts is realistic only in the area of specific communication tools, such as artificial languages of the type used in computer sciences, because only such languages can be regarded as fully compatible or can be manipulated with the aim of reaching full compatibility.

3. Translation is a process of substituting arbitrary sign sequences by arbitrary TL sign sequences. This definition is relevant to MT. In the practical testing of MT procedures organized according to the principle of substitution techniques, it has, however, become apparent rather quickly that only in rare cases is it feasible to translate natural-language texts on the basis of syntactic and lexical one-to-one correspondences (Blatt et al., 1985; Schmitz, 1986). It is a fundamental feature of interlingual transfer that no language pair is isomorphic and that, in going from SL to TL, the translator must take into consideration language-pair specific structural and socio-

cultural divergences forcing him to adopt compensatory transfer strategies (Reiss/Vermeer, 1984; Holz-Mänttäri, 1984). Thus, any translating activity depends on conditions and prerequisites which have provoked Jakobson's famous characterization of interlingual transfer operations as attempts to obtain "equivalence in difference" (1966) and which have led Nida to define the aim of translating, in a meanwhile no less famous formula, as the striving for the "closest natural equivalent" (1964). Concerning interlingual transfer, structural divergencies mean that SL-analytical and TL-synthetical operations, as a rule, do not run parallel. The functional units constituting the SL text are normally not suitable for direct (surface structure) transfer. As a result, they must be reorganized in such a way as to harmonize with TL rules and norms. This procedure requires a highly subtle and textually differentiated restructuring competence or transfer competence (Hönig/Kußmaul, 1982). A lower-level competence is sufficient only in cases where the computer is confronted with texts marked by a controlled syntax and a controlled lexis, i.e. texts consisting of interlingually standardized and unambiguous text segments (text modules). But such delightful transfer conditions are – even in the realm of syntactically and lexically restricted LSP communication – the exception rather than the rule. Contrary to artificial languages, natural language is, by its very nature, not a hermetically closed communication tool (as presently developed by experts in "linguistic engineering") which can be adapted to the rigorous functional principle of the computer (Wilss, 1988a). Finiteness is alien to any natural language. Natural language must be understood and accepted as a multifunctional, dynamic, variability-oriented phenomenon, rather than as a statically determined entity or as a binary code which permits only two mutually exclusive alternatives and confines the translator to interlingual transformulation processes. Hence, translation is basically a decision process (Vinay, 1966; Levy, 1967; Kußmaul, 1986; Wilss, 1988b). The result of such decision processes is largely determined by linguistic structures, textual configurations, receptor-oriented considerations, and – last but not least – by the personality of the translator, his attitude toward the text to be transferred, his text-analytical capabilities and the level of his translational creativity. I shall come back to this point later on in more detail.

What has been said so far is a good starting-point for illustrating the methodical dilemma between the argumentative frame of reference of translation theory over the last 2000 years (since Cicero) and modern TS. Störig, in his anthology on the history of translation theory (1969, continued by Wilss, 1981b) has convincingly shown that the international discussion of translation problems has not proceeded in a straightforward, logically plausible fashion, but must be seen as a conglomeration of various, often diametrically opposed theoretical viewpoints and methodological postulates. In a simplified manner, one could say that the discussion of translation theory has in the past concentrated on two problem areas:

1. the theoretical problem of interlingual translatability vs. untranslatability,

2. the methodological problems involved in the establishing of equivalence criteria and in formulating principled translation strategies and transfer techniques.

The aspect of translatability, partial translatability and untranslatability of texts has received adequate treatment only relatively late in the history of translation theory, namely in the Romantic period. This is not incidental, because it was in the Romantic period that national peculiarities and intralingual idiosyncrasies aroused widespread interest, thus giving new impetus to, and providing new perspectives for, the discussion of transfer-theoretical issues. Prior to the Romantic period, the discussion of translation problems had concentrated on the question of which translation norm was most appropriate to achieve an optimal translation result.

The long-standing interest in methodological questions is mainly due to the fact that it was, above all, practising translators who were involved in this dispute. They carried on their argumentation over the principles and postulates of translation mainly against the background of the clarification and justification of their respective translation approach, and less for the purpose of developing a translation-theoretical frame of reference.

Interesting as these notions may be, it is obvious that, strictly speaking, this search for a translation-processual frame of reference was notorious for its circularity, displaying, in the last analysis, widespread reluctance to provide objectified solutions for translation problems. This circularity can be gathered from the fact that, ultimately, the argumentation has always come back to its starting point, namely the bifurcation of translation methods into the postulates of "ut interpres" (faithful, SL-oriented translation) and "ut orator" (free, TL-oriented translation, including the semantic and stylistic TL paraphrasing of SL texts) – a methodogical controversy which originated with Cicero. By polarizing these two transfer principles he articulated two basic positions which largely dominated the theoretical discussion of translation problems right into the middle of the 20th century.

On the whole, the history of translation theory reflects very speculative and impressionistic attitudes. The relative stagnation of the discussion of translation problems can be regarded as being indicative of the fact that translation theory, in its historical dimensions, failed to develop an adequate concept of its subject-matter. It was unable to distinguish clearly between factual, descriptive statements and normative, evaluative statements. As a result, it was unable (or unwilling, as the case may be) to open new theoretical vistas and thus to expand the spectrum of translation issues. Translation theory could have changed this inherently deplorable state of affairs at the beginning of the 19th century, if it had taken up von Humboldt's concept of interlanguage comparison, using it for the development of a translation-theoretical frame of reference. Von Humboldt's probing questions about the character of natural languages and the basic principle of human communication, questions which ultimately amount to the problem of integrating universal and monadic aspects of language theory, fell, however, into oblivion in the course of the 19th century. This is the result of the fact that, in the post-Humboldt period, translation theorists revitalized the notorious controversy as to whether a translation should be faithful or whether it should be free.

Thus, another century had to pass by until the reasoning powers of the traditional translation-theoretical arguments were more or less exhausted. It was not until the middle of the 20th century that a new translation-theoretical concept became visible, aiming at an unprejudiced observation and registration of transfer-process oriented and transfer-result oriented facts and thus creating the preconditions for the formation of a new empirical, descriptive, and explanative frame of reference. The new theoretical attitude is characterized by the de-mystification of translation theory and the emergence of an analytical treatment of translation problems. This new development, which George Steiner, in his book *After Babel* (1975), tried in vain to stop, culminated in the formulation of the question of how the translator must proceed linguistically in order to achieve the following two targets:

1. interlingual text synchronization taking account of the specific communicative goals of the SL text author and the specific needs of the TL text recipient (Snell-Hornby, 1986),

2. compensation of interlingual syntactic, semantic, and sociocultural divergencies (Nida/Reyburn, 1981).

The formulation of these two questions signalled, at the same time, the end of the often excessive overestimation of the language-behavior determining character of the interdependence between the linguistic repertoire and the worldview of a language community. This philosophy was now replaced by a more pragmatic and more dynamic concept of language for which Wandruszka has created the term "instrumental permeability" (1973). According to him, language is a functionally organized, polysystemic structure which possesses not only idiosyncratic, but also universal properties and, accordingly, allows the interlingual representation of concrete communicative events.

The statement by Coseriu (1975) that all languages are contrary (konträr) but not contradictory (kontradiktorisch), has also turned out to be an important boost for TS. The notion that natural languages are in principle commensurate implies that extralinguistic reality exists independently of language-specific concepts and structures. It is true, however, that individual languages codify extralinguistic reality rather differently. But these codification differences are – at least in the semantic realm of linguistic communication – of peripheral rather than of central importance. To deduce from this phenomenon a theory of general untranslatability or to hypothesize, as Quine (1966) has done, about the radical indeterminacy of translation, is inadmissible for the following reason: It is relatively easy to show that this type of "ontological relativity" largely ignores, in an almost anti-empirical fashion, the situational dimension of texts and the feasibility of imaginative translation work, thus raising a fringe phenomenon of interlingual communication to the level of a theory of principal untranslatability (Mounin 1963). Contrary to the rather narrow concept of translation revealed by Quine and the representatives of the theory of untranslatability, modern linguistics maintains that basically everything can be expressed in all languages or, to quote Wittgenstein, that all languages are "complete". Each language can cover, at least tendentially, all communicational needs of a language community, even those which originally may have been alien to it.

This "change of paradigm" (Kuhn, 1962) from a speculative translation theory to empirically founded TS is terminologically reflected in the emergence of the term "Übersetzungswissenschaft" (science of translation). In the German-speaking area, this term has had the status of a scientific term since the early 1960s (Kade, 1963); its coinage is, however, much older. It stems from Schleiermacher who as early as 1813, possibly under the influence of von Humboldt's language philosophy, demanded the development of a (hermeneutically based) "Übersetzungswissenschaft".

The fact that in the early 1960s a scientific frame of reference for the investigation of translation problems became visible is documented by the appearance of Nida's by now classical book, *Toward a Science of Translating* (1964). At the same time, this book, with its

deliberately cautious title, is an indication of the difficulties encountered by TS in constituting an autonomous field of research
which can clearly be marked off from other disciplines of modern
descriptive language comparison, such as contrastive linguistics,
confrontative linguistics, including Wandruszka's concept of mul-
tilateral translation comparison (1969).

The difficulties encountered by modern TS in formulating and
delimiting a homogeneous field of research were aggravated by
two facts:

1. Translation activity can be motivated by widely differing linguistic as well as communicative targets. The multifariousness of
   transfer goals has considerably hampered the development of a
   "unified theory of translation" (Nida, 1976, 78) with clearly
   definable and defendable research objectives.

2. The attempts to develop a sound methodology for translation research are, at least in some quarters, still being looked upon with
   scepticism or are even ignored altogether (Herbst et al., 1979).
   Whatever the reason may be, these sceptics tend to ignore the
   fact that TS, at least in its modern, linguistico-semiotic manifesta-
   tion, is, as stated before, a fairly young and methodologically
   still somewhat unstable field of research (Wilss, 1977/1982). This
   is a state of affairs which TS shares with other modern linguistic
   subdisciplines such as psycholinguistics, sociolinguistics, text linguistics and speech act theory which will probably play a more
   outstanding role in the further development of TS than has been
   the case so far (Wilss, 1988a).

TS, in its modern appearance, is approximately as old as MT.
There is now fairly widespread consensus that Weaver's famous
memorandum of 1947 to Wiener constitutes the official prelude to
MT research (Wiener, 1955). Unlike MT research, modern TS has
nothing comparable to offer, unless one regards Nida's book *Bible
Translation and the Analysis of Principles and Procedures with Special
Reference to Aboriginal Languages* (1947), the prerunner of his already
mentioned book of 1964, as a scientific pacemaker. It should be
noted in this context, however, that Nida's 1947 book did not have
the same impact as the Weaver memorandum or Chomsky's book,
Syntactic Structures (1957), which was equated for some time, rather

euphorically, with a Copernican revolution in linguistic thinking. Neither has Fedorov's book *Vvedenie v teoriju perevoda* (Introduction to the Theory of Translation, [1]1953, meanwhile, with a different title, in its fourth edition), gained the status of a translation-scientific primer. The reason for this is perhaps, apart from its publication in Russian, that it holds an interim position between traditional, philologically-oriented translation theory and modern, linguistically based TS.

It can be stated pretty safely that translation research has meanwhile left behind this transitional period. Nevertheless, its scientific autonomy is, as stated above, not yet fully accepted, and it is perhaps not uninteresting to trace the difficulties confronting translation research in formulating a theoretically and methodically sound concept of TS:

1. It is, above all for the outsider, not immediately evident that there is a substantial and theoretically justifiable need for the scientific investigation of the translation process and the translation product. Normally, for the reader of translations and for the practising translator, it is sufficient to know that one can perform translational activities if one possesses an adequately differentiated linguistic, extralinguistic and sociocultural knowledge in two languages. Moreover, those who report on activities in the field of translation research must wade through masses of often pretentious, glutinous, heavily metaphorical or extremely abstract prose, seeking the flash of insight, the buried diamond of evaluation; the key to the progress we are told is under way now.

2. Translation is aimed at functional (or communicative) equivalence between SL text and TL text (Koller, 1979). In the search for, and in the assessment of, translation equivalence, the practising translator relies mainly or even exclusively on his translational experience. Despite all efforts – and these efforts have been manifold and they should not be trivialized – the discussion on translation equivalence is still characterized by relatively global, definitionally difficult-to-grasp concepts. This is obvious if one looks at the current equivalence terminology which is to some extent

characterized by what Lefevere has called "lack of scientific ecology" (1978,8). There we have, among other terms, functional equivalence (Jäger, 1973), equivalence in difference (Jakobson, 1966), maintenance (retention) of translation invariance on the content level (Kade, 1968), equality of textual effect (Koller, 1972), illusionist vs. anti-illusionist translation (Levy, 1969), closest natural equivalent (Nida, 1964), formal correspondence vs. dynamic equivalence (Nida, 1964), stylistic equivalence (Popovic, 1971), functional invariance (Roganova, 1971), communicative equivalence (Reiss, 1976), pragmatic equivalence (Wilss, 1980a; "pragmatic" understood here within a semiotic frame of reference as a term describing and regulating the communicative relations between the sender and the receptor of a text).

3. The predominantly subjective element in the qualitative evaluation of translation products is probably interconnected with difficulties in establishing an objective framework for the measurement of translation competence. Hence, applied TS finds it extremely cumbersome to define learning targets and to develop operational criteria for testing learning progress in the field of translation (Königs, 1987; Nord, 1987). TS has failed to provide satisfactory answers to the question of professional minimum qualifications, because unified performance criteria are largely non-existent in the translation field. Translation procedures are highly diversified activities including LSP translation, literary translation, Bible translation, and film-dubbing, to name only a few. In addition, it is necessary to distinguish between TL/SL transfer activities which are as yet predominant in translation practice, and SL/TL translation activities, which, however, are gaining ground in the translation profession. It is also understandable that it is, above all, the translation practitioner who has, time and again, expressed doubts as to the relevance and applicability of a theory of translation in general and a theory of translation equivalence in particular. In doing so, he refers implicitly to the so-called "milliped argument" (the milliped loses its natural ability of locomotion the very moment it begins to reflect on the complicated mechanism of its

locomotion apparatus). Thus, it is not surprising that the translation practitioner prefers to rely on his translational intuition if he
has to make a statement as to whether in his opinion a translation
is adequate, less adequate or inadequate (Wilss, 1988a).

The sceptical attitude toward the usefulness of the scientific
investigation of transfer phenomena is doubtless the explanation
for the relative insignificance of TS in the mind of the public. TS
obviously so far has been unable to convincingly demonstrate the
social meaning of translation research to the public (Wilss, 1987).
In other words, TS in the eyes of the public, does not really represent a topic which could not be integrated into other disciplines or
subdisciplines within the framework of the humanities or social
sciences. TS, to be sure, does cover – or at any rate should cover –
all translationally relevant problems under theological, philosophical, aesthetic, ethnographical, anthropological, sociocultural, semiotic, communicative and – more recently – even under technological and behavioral aspects, but it is this very diversity of research perspectives which stands in the way of working out a
homogeneous translation research paradigm.

In addition, there is, at least among non-experts, the widespread
opinion that it is quite possible to be an efficient professional
translator (less so an interpreter) without formal training, the argumentation being that, just as a native speaker can efficiently use
his native tongue without explicit knowledge of its syntactic, lexical and pragmatic rule systems, it must be possible to make adequate translations without theoretical investigations into what is
going on in the course of a translation process and how an adequate
translation is actually being brought about. And it is indeed an
irrefutable fact that there do exist persons who possess a natural
gift for translation or who have qualified as expert translators by
means of self-teaching methods. Those persons are, however, at
any rate in the field of LSP texts, rare birds.

Translation is, apart from the reproduction of phraseologically
petrified and interlingually highly standardized text elements
(Wilss, 1989a), a form of linguistic performance requiring subtle

abilities of SL/TL text synchronization on the syntactic, semantic and pragmatic text level (Wilss, 1980a). The most convincing evidence is provided, as indicated above, by MT. MT research has so far attempted in vain to decipher the "black box" of the translation process (Wilss, 1980b). As a result, it has turned out to be inadequate in all cases where the transfer process cannot be reduced to the linear replacement of SL text segments by corresponding TL text segments. Uneasiness about the ultimate success of MT is interconnected with the principle of "tertium datur": language usage simply cannot be treated exhaustively within a concept of binary oppositions.

The failure by MT research to handle translating as an intelligent operation and to work out simulation procedures covering all or at least all major dimensions of the intertextual transfer is also due to another factor: The text to be translated faces the translator as a "silent object" which he must first penetrate receptively and then reproduce in the TL. In doing so, he is entirely dependent on his own mental resources, because in most cases there is no contact between himself and the SL author. Hence, the interlingual transfer is not embedded in a feedback circle. Exceptions, especially in the realm of literary translation, confirm the rule. Whether the translator has been semantically and stylistically successful in his transfer efforts cannot, as a rule, be stated with an absolute degree of certainty. Every translation is essentially an interaction-free, monological act, or a case of "one-way communication".

Incidentally, this is the explanation for the great difficulties in establishing objective criteria for translation criticism. The translation critic is confronted with the co-presence of two interrelated text occurrences, the SL text and the TL text which can be regarded as a "meta-text" of the SL text. His task is to ascertain the level of translation equivalence between these two texts, thereby taking account of the intention of the SL author and the expectation of the TL receptor (Koller, 1974). However, often, e.g. in literary translation, the translation critic behaves in a different manner: He "starts by positing his or her norms as absolute and systematically proceeds to damn each and every deviation from them rather than to try to establish what norms have guided the literary translator in his or her work" (Lefevere, 1978,3; see also Toury, 1980; Frank, 1986). This is to say that translation criticism is in the same dilemma as translation equivalence concerning the lack of an objective – or objectifiable – frame of reference; therefore subjective judgements, although undesirable, are largely unavoidable. The objectivity of translation criticism is, strictly speaking, limited to cases where the critic can locate, describe and explain transfer errors on a correct/incorrect basis, i.e. where he restricts his activities to what Gipper (1971) has ingeniously called the "langue-context", including the systemic aspects of text production, text perception and text reproduction.

It follows from what has been said that TS needs the same kind of explicit set of postulates which were accomplished for theoretical linguistics as early as 1926 by Bloomfield and expanded by Chomsky as of 1957 within the framework of "Generative Transformational Grammar". It is a well-known fact that scientific progress does not consist of simply heaping up data material, but rather of the formulation of objective issues, of the empirical testing of adequate research methods and of the presentation of verifiable or, for that matter, falsifiable research results. Hence, modern TS has tried, and is still trying, to develop a research concept, thus following up the transition in modern linguistics from a langue-oriented to a parole-oriented, or from a sentence-oriented to a text-oriented research paradigm (Thiel, 1981; Neubert, 1987). This shift of emphasis is, above all, obvious in the increased attention being given by modern TS to semiotic aspects of human communication (Wilss, 1980a). The incorporation of the semiotic dimension into translation research is plausible because the translator does not translate isolated words or sentences (unless a sentence has text status), but texts (Weinrich, 1966). A central task of TS therefore is the analytical description and explanation of texts, because the communicative analysis of the SL text is one of the decisive "felicity conditions" for semantically, functionally and pragmatically successful transfer operations.

The text-orientedness of TS has helped to launch a new translation theory which aims at the explication of the communicative
interrelatedness between SL text, type of text, translator and receptor of the TL text (Snell-Hornby, 1986). By placing the concept of
the interlingual tertium comparationis (which, by the way, explains
Nida's replacement of the term TL by receptor language (1964)), in
the center of translation research (Coseriu, 1981b), modern TS has
conceived a number of translation-relevant text typologies.

This subdivision of the text cosmos into separate areas is important for TS, because it provokes the question whether one should
not give up the idea of creating a unified, comprehensive theory of
translation and replace this goal by working toward a number of
text-type oriented translation theories (Newmark, 1981).

Text-type oriented TS has rather early parcelled out the various
areas of research. Thus, Jumpelt (1961) and Pinchuk (1977) have
confined themselves to the presentation of translation problems
arising in connection with LSP texts. Their books are, as it were,
the counterparts to the works by Kloepfer (1967), Levy (1969),
Meschonnic (1973), de Beaugrande (1978), Holmes at al. (1978),
Zuber (1980) and Rose (1981), who have concentrated on the investigation of translation problems in literary texts. The trend toward
concentrating on one text-type can also be observed in the book by
Reiss, *Texttyp und Übersetzungsmethode. Der operative Text* (1976).

Like all classificatory efforts, the classification of texts with a
view to establishing text-type specific transfer criteria can clarify
the relation between text-type and translation method only in general, idealizing fashion. It seems that, at least for the time being,
text-oriented TS must sidetrack the delicate question of discovering
text-specific and text-type specific text constituents and establishing text-type specific transfer regularities. Much more important,
and probably more fruitful, is the empirical approach of text-oriented TS proceeding from individual texts (Schultze, 1987). It is their
target to offer the translation student and the practising translator
transfer directives and thus to objectify his decisions in favor of a

specific transfer strategy. Hence, text-oriented TS falls, strictly speaking, into the category of applied translation research; it recognizes the text to be translated as the product of a situationally embedded text-manufacturing procedure in which syntactic and lexical text elements are assembled according to the semantic, functional and pragmatic notions of the SL text author. This entails a research program combining four interconnected research aspects:

1. the linguistic (i.e. syntactic and lexical) analysis of the SL text structure,

2. the provision of a semantically, functionally and pragmatically satisfactory explanation of the distribution of lexical and syntactic text elements,

3. the deduction of adequate transfer strategies,

4. the establishment of intratextual and – in the long run – of text-type specific criteria for the evaluation of the translation product.

This leads to the conclusion that text-oriented TS must be regarded as a partly hermeneutic, partly analytical field of research which tries to tackle translation problems in a dynamic fashion, thus complying with Nida's demand for "dynamic equivalence" in interlingual transfer (1964). Text-oriented TS seeks answers to the question of the conditions and the feasibility of efficient text transfer and the semiotic balance between SL text and TL text.

It should be remembered in this context that TS is by its very nature an undertaking which is determined by the perpetual interplay of descriptive, explanative and normative research aspects. As in chess, to exploit de Saussure's famous simile for the illustration of translation research problems – translation is characterized by the combination of obligatory and optional, by constant and variable text-elements.

These elements are joined together, thus making possible the communicative double-strategy of "rule-governed behavior" and "rule-governed creativity" (Göttert 1979). This is to say that SL and TL text elements normally do not stand in a one-to-one, but in a one-to-many relation, allowing the translator to select between several TL elements of more or less the same qualitative rank. This is a state of affairs which forces text-oriented TS to move away from model-theoretic argumentation and to focus its activities on a research program including neighboring disciplines such as contrastive linguistics, comparative linguistics, denotational, connotational and collocational semantics, stylistics, communication sciences, psycholinguistics, sociolinguistics, computer linguistics, text linguistics, literary studies, reception aesthetics, semiotics and, last but not least, cognitive psychology (Hönig, 1986; Wilss, 1988a).

The latter aspect is of outstanding significance, because a translator may adopt a specific transfer strategy, according to the structure, content and function of the text he is confronted with. In an LSP text, for example, the sender/recipient relationship is symmetrical, provided, as indicated earlier, linguistic and extra-linguistic or referential knowledge are levelled out among the two interlocutors. The production and perception of LSP texts is primarily object-oriented. LSP texts are largely recipient-independent, if we look at their semantic, functional and pragmatic dimension. LSP texts are aimed at the description and explanation of scientific and technological topics. Therefore they are largely "depersonalized". This tendency is most conspicuous in the formalized languages of mathematics, physics, chemistry and electronic data processing. Formalized languages of this type are abstract sign systems; their job is to facilitate the representation of more or less complex relations in a non-linguistic functional system. The hermeneutic interpretation of such texts turns out to be useless as a method of decoding LSP texts. The function of LSP texts is not to decipher unknown things by activating inborn capabilities of divination, but to disseminate scientific and technological knowledge through the analytical approach to LSP texts in a specific field of research and application (Arntz/Picht, 1982). The principled subject/object separation in the presentation of scientific and technological knowledge reflects itself linguistically: LSP texts contain conventionalized textual elements on the lexical and syntactic level (Wilss,

1981a). Seen against this background, LSP texts display a specific communicative calculus. As such, LSP texts are an important component of what Mumford has called the "mega-machine" (1978), paving the way for the transition into the cybernetic phase of industrial civilization. LSP texts operate on certain sets of pre-structured and, as a consequence, predictable text patterns which permit the derivation of LSP text constitution rules. They can be thought of as recurrent formats, or, as Coseriu would say, as a form of "repetitive speech" (wiederholte Rede) (1988), which gradually becomes internalized in the same sense of Lacan's concept of an "imprinting process" (1973).

LSP text patterns possess an instructive quality both for the text sender and for the text recipient. Hence, they are an important factor in the writing of LSP texts and in the ascertainment of reversible standard equivalents in the field of LSP translation: If X in SL, then Y in TL. If Y in TL, then X in SL. The surface-structure standardization of LSP texts is alleviated by another factor. In LSP texts five types of argumentation are predominant, the constative, causal, conditional, concessive and purposive type of argumentation (Wilss, 1985).

For the above-mentioned five types of argumentation, there is a framework of three modes of expression, the paratactic mode, the hypotactic mode and nominalizations (often introduced with the aid of prepositions). These modes of representation can be regarded as psychologically real syntactic configurations. On the other hand, the relation between text sender and text recipient, an outstanding subject-matter in text linguistics, is asymmetrical in a literary text. This is to say that the recipient of a literary text does not, at least not always, respond to a particular text in the manner intended by the text sender. This is due to the fact that in the approach to, and in the understanding of, a literary text, the text sender and the text recipient may adopt quite different strategies. In many cases, a literary text is deliberately organized in such a way as to compel the text recipient to interpret a particular literary text, to make the implicit structures or elements of a literary text explicit, to read as it were, his own concept of the thing meant into this text. In doing so, the text recipient can only succeed if he is ready to stop falling back upon his habitual methods of text decoding and to develop new methods of contextualization and sense combinations.

"A work of literature . . . is not to be identified with a text as a fixed object. . . . The reader 'realizes' the text, links up things which are not explicitly connected, makes guesses, fills in gaps, constructs points of view, creates tensions . . ." (Hrusovski 1976,2). "Da hilft dir kein Code. Du mußt dir die Nachricht selbst erfinden" (A code will not be helpful. You must invent the message for yourself), says Riedler in a poem "Nachricht von den Malediven" (Süddeutsche Zeitung, August 1, 1981). This statement clearly indicates – and the utopian attempts at positing literary texts within a framework of generative text grammar seem to confirm this – that it is to all intents and purposes impossible to reduce the investigations of literary texts in such a way as to comprise only features which can be analyzed and translated on a rigorously linguistic basis.

What is required here is a search for meaning and symbolism, a way to establish poetry's ties with human experience, a way to find and express specific value systems, a concern for poetry in the context of society. The solution of this task is hampered by the fact that literary texts are characterized by "underdetermination" (Weinrich, Süddeutsche Zeitung, September 1, 1979), a phenomenon for which, according to Weinrich, the theorists of literary studies have coined many terms: "indeterminacy" (Unbestimmtheit), "empty patches" (Leerstellen), or "holes in the text" (Löcher im Text). It was Sklovskij who, as early as 1916, called the language of poetry an artificial language or a twisted language (eine "verbogene" Sprache), forcing the reader to adopt a strategy of hesitation which may considerably slow down the process of reception of a literary text. This implies not only that literary texts are different from other texts, but also that the translation of literary texts confronts the translation practitioner with many difficulties, probably with more difficulties than, say, the translation of LSP texts (this is a hypothesis which was vehemently contradicted by Soellner (1980)). What the literary translator must have at his disposal is a specific flair for creative translation or, for that matter, a specific type of translation creativity. Now creative translation is an enormously complex and elusive concept which cannot be discussed here at length. Strictly speaking, translating is not a creative, but a re-creative act of linguistic performance. Translation is never a "creatio ex nihilo", but the doubly rule-bound reproduction of a given text. Nevertheless creative translation is, as any type of creativity, a dynamic concept. This is particularly true of literary texts. The dynamic component of the literary translation process manifests itself not in original text production, but in the ability to develop – in simultaneous confrontation with an SL text and the lexical and syntactic inventories of a TL – single-text specific transfer methods (not so much a text-type oriented transfer methodology), leading to a congenial transfer result.

Here the question arises – and this question is of particular interest to somebody who is heavily involved in the training of translators – whether literary texts can sensibly be integrated into a framework of systematic translation teaching. Against the background of applied translation research, it seems that one can, at least provisionally, distinguish four areas of scientific activity (Wilss, 1977/1982):

1. the description, explanation, weighing and elimination of translation difficulties in going from one particular SL to one particular TL (Nord, 1987),

2. the development of learner-oriented translation teaching strategies (mainly for the area of L_2/L_1 transfer) under the aspect of the systematic development of operational "minimax-strategies" (Levy 1967) with an optimal input/output relation,

3. the development of a translation-specific concept of error analysis (as a precondition for translation criticism) (Wilss, 1989b),

4. the development of a methodology for the objective or near-objective evaluation of translation products (Rose, 1987).

Of these four research areas, 1 and 2 can be assigned to the prospectively oriented branch of TS; their topic is the investigation of the transfer leading from the SL text to the TL text; 3 and 4, on the other hand, fall under the category of retrospectively oriented TS. Their operational basis are translation products, their target is the reconstruction of the translation process and the elimination of syntactic, semantic and pragmatic deficiencies in the translation product; 1 and 2 on the one side, and 3 and 4 on the other, stand in a complementary relationship. All four research areas can be integrated into a comprehensive concept of applied translation research (Bühler, 1984/86). It must aim at the systematic improvement of the transfer competence of the individual translator student and, by teaching him text-related transfer methods and transfer techniques, at providing him with an optimal basis for starting his practical professional work (Wilss, 1983).

SUPPLEMENT *

The original version of the critical survey above was written in 1981; in 1989, significant research updates were added. The crucial orientation of the essay was, in keeping with the field of translation theory as it was then, text-linguistic. In the meantime a trend which was already recognizable then in translation theory has intensified into a cognitive viewpoint. This trend, which is only broadly outlined in the text above, has opened up the question how translation is carried out as an intertextually determined transfer process, and what role is played by the relevant factors in the translation process: the text and its author, the translator and his areas of knowledge and imagery which guide the transfer, as well as the recipient of the text and his qualitative expectations. The positions of the persons meeting in a translation situation can diverge considerably. Every translation situation represents a complex constellation of roles, the scientific elaboration of which raises problems of objectivization. For the translator it is a matter of activating

---

* Translation by Professor George Thomas, Coordinator of Linguistics at McMaster University

disposable knowledge (epistemological knowledge) and orientational knowledge (procedural knowledge) in the correct relationship to each other. Under disposable knowledge are to be subsumed the linguistic and extralinguistic knowledge potential which the translator can call upon. Orientational knowledge on the other hand concerns the capability of employing the appropriate translation methods and techniques for a successful translation behavior.

He who behaves linguistically – and translation is a specific form of linguistic behavior – has one goal in view. In the context of translation behavior this goal is the production of a pragmatic balance between the original and the target text. On the translator thus devolves the task of determining the conditions for a textual transfer adequate to the situation against the background of what is textually intended and from that of drawing the right conclusions about the translation processes and of substantiating them evaluatively.

The translator can indeed make the translation behavior connections for the originator of the text, for himself and for the receptor transparent only when he has learned, in the framework of more or less complex (and correspondingly mentally more or less absorbing) information-treating procedures, to recognize textual structures and functions and to devise the strategies of textual transfer which promise success for their rendering in the target language.

Such considerations amount to a gradual planning, in which all the dimensions relative to the translation process (the subject matter, function, pragmatics and the surface of the text) are measured cognitively, in order to establish the most suitable route possible for reaching the main goal of the translator. For that one needs a rational attack, whose explicit goal it must be, to decipher the notorious "black box" of the translator in the framework of the possible by means of a "turning inward" and with the help of psychological concepts to bring to light the mental strategies and processes basic to translating on the basis of a model of information-processing.

The science of translation thus forms a bridge to Wilhelm von Humboldt, who might be viewed as the founder of a cognitive translation theory, if the form of language comparison developed by him had been continued in a way relevant to the science of translation. It forms thereby a link with Wilhelm Wundt, who with his thesis of the "internal reality" of language activity anticipated much of what is discussed today by cognitive psychology in the context of the study of mental representations.

With such considerations the science of translation still stands right at the beginning of a new phase of interests to direct our knowledge. There is not yet an exhaustive theory of conscious experience, and it is a good question, whether there ever will be. In any case there can be doubts, when one thinks for example of the discrepancy between cognitive claims of value and the results of research in the field of artificial intelligence and machine translation. A comprehensive monograph on the theory of cognitive systems in general and the cognitive theory of translation in particular will not be available for some time.

Translation is by its nature a transitory process. The translator achieves the translation from the textual configuration of the original language to that of the target language taking into account the interlingual "tertium comparationis," which can be viewed as the Archimedes point of any translation process. If one looks at translation as a transitory process, the original text represents the initial state; this initial state is not properly defined in the sense of a "well-defined problem", but only approximately at best. The same is true, mutatis mutandis, for the target text: it represents the final state in the translation process. Even this final state is not properly, at least not comprehensively, but only partially defined, as is shown by the endless discussions about the concept of translation equivalence. The best proof of this is the fact that in the rendering of an original text one has to reckon as a rule with several equivalent variants, which can be designated as intralinguistic paraphrases of each other in the target language.

The reformulation of the original text into the target language raises difficulties, wherever the translator cannot translate literally – in the sense of lexical, idiomatic and syntactic one-to-one correspondences, but must translate non-literally. These difficulties, as indicated, he tries to overcome with the help of his declarative and procedural stock of knowledge in the form of "internal language acts." For these acts he drafts an overall plan, which can consist of several partial plans synchronised with and feeding back on each other, in the framework of his capacity for action as a translator, that is his competence at problem-solving, his competence for decision-making, his creativity and his intuition.

As translation activity shows, several procedures in translation are to be anticipated more than others; the translation process is therefore a stochastic process. The conduct of the translator is based to a certain degree on a system. This system, which must be studied in more detail in the context of modern systems theory, does not have an absolute but only a statistical validity; it is possible, because – just like unilingual communication – even interlingual communication is rule-governed. This regulatoriness allows the translator, in the framework of the spectrum of the possibilities of the target language, to develop certain modes of conduct, which we can operate successfully in the framework of certain translation constellations. The more modes of conduct he masters, the more control he has over his original text, the more rational, economic, routine and calculable is the translator's employment of his linguistic data.

From this emerge wide-reaching conclusions for the teaching of translation. These fall into the area of competence of the applied science of translation, which must be aware that it cannot behave more scientifically than is possible and meaningful from the point of view of the nature and the complexity of its object area. Its scientificity must be a means to an end, not an end in itself, and it must present its perceptions in a way which is suitable, productive and fulfillable for teachers and students alike.

If the teaching of translation keeps to these precepts, it can make statements which will effect a "transfer of training" and help to fill the wide gap existing between translation theory and practice. However, we must also recognize that in the area of language use, whether inter- or intra-lingual, there are limits to objectivization, and that one has to reckon with points of uncertainty, which no teaching method, however subtle, can dispose of, but must accept as an intrinsic and indispensable element of communicative inter-action.

BIBLIOGRAPHY

de Beaugrande R., *Factors in a theory of poetic translating*. Assen. 1978.

Bloomfield L., "A set of Postulates for the Science of Language; the Status of Linguistics as a Science or Linguistics as an Exact Science." *Language* 2, 153-164. 1926.

Cassirer P., *Stylistics as Pragmatics or the Linguistic Fallacy*. Ms. 1978.

Chomsky N., *Syntactic Structures*. The Hague. 1957.

Coseriu E., "Die sprachlichen (und die anderen) Universalien." In: Schlieben-Lange B. (ed.), *Sprachtheorie*. Hamburg, 127-161. 1975.

Coseriu E., "Kontrastive Linguistik und Übersetzungstheorie: ihr Verhältnis zueinander." In: Kühlwein W., Thome G., Wilss W. (eds.), *Kontrastive Linguistik und Übersetzungswissenschaft*. München, 183-199. 1981a.

Coseriu E., "Falsche und richtige Fragestellungen in der Übersetzungstheorie." In: Wilss W., 27-47. 1981b.

Coseriu E., *Einführung in die allgemeine Sprachwissenschaft*. Tübingen. 1988

Fedorov A.V., *Vvedenie v teoriju perevoda* (Introduction to the Theory of Translation). Moscow. 1953.

Fritsch G., "Die Trivialliteratur und ihre Stellung heute." *Universitas* 6, 629-636. 1981.

Gipper H., "Polysemie, Homonymie und Kontext." In: Schweisthal K.G. (ed.), *Grammatik, Kybernetik, Kommunikation. Festschrift für Alfred Hoppe*. Bonn, 202-214. 1971.

Göttert K.-H., "Regelbefolgung, Regeldurchbrechung, Regelerneuerung." *Zeitschrift für Germanistische Linguistik* 7.2, 151-166. 1979

Herbst Th. et al., *Grimm's Grandchildren. Current Topics in German Linguistics*. London/New York. 1979.

Holmes J.S. et al. (eds.), *Literature and Translation. New Perspectives in Literary*

Studies. Leuven. 1978.

Hrushovski B., "Segmentation and Motivation in the Text Continuum of Literary Prose. The First Episode of 'War and Peace'." *Papers on Poetics and Semiotics* 5, Tel-Aviv University. 1976.

Jäger G., "Invarianz und Transferierbarkeit." In: Neubert A./Kade O. (eds.), *Neue Beiträge zu Fragen der Übersetzungswissenschaft*. Frankfurt, 47-59. 1973.

Jakobson R., "On Linguistic Aspects of Translation." In: Brower R.A. (ed.), *On Translation*. New York, 232-239. [2]1966.

Jumpelt R.W., *Die Übersetzung naturwissenschaftlicher und techni scher Literatur*. Berlin. 1961.

Kade O., "Aufgaben der Übersetzungswissenschaft." *Fremdsprachen*, 83-94. 1963.

Kade O., "Zufall und Gesetzmäßigkeit in der Übersetzung." *Beihefte zur Zeitschrift Fremdsprachen* I. Leipzig. 1968.

Kloepfer R., *Die Theorie der literarischen Übersetzung. Romanisch-deutscher Sprachraum*. München. 1967.

Koller W., *Grundprobleme der Übersetzungstheorie*. Bern. 1972.

Koller W., "Anmerkungen zu Definitionen des Übersetzungs"vorgangs" und der Übersetzungskritik." In: Wilss W./Thome G. (eds.), *Aspekte der theoretischen, sprachenpaarbezogenen und angewandten Sprachwissenschaft (Übersetzungswissenschaft)*, vol. I. Saarbrücken/Heidelberg, 35-55. 1974.

Kuhn Th.S., *The Structure of Scientific Revolutions*. Chicago. 1962.

Lacan J., *Les quatre concepts fondamentaux de la psychanalyse*. Paris. 1973.

Lefevere A., *Programmatic Second Thoughts on "Literary" and "Translation." Or: Where do we go from here?* Ms. 1978.

Levy J., "Translation as a Decision Process." *To Honor Roman Jakobson. Essays on the Occasion of his 70th Birthday*, vol II. The Hague, 1171-1182. 1967.

Levy J., *Die literarische Übersetzung. Theorie einer Kunstgattung*. Frankfurt. 1969.

Meschonnic H., *Pour une poétique de la traduction*. Paris. 1973.

Mounin G., *Les problèmes théoriques de la traduction*. Paris. 1963.

Mumford L., *Mythos der Maschine. Kultur, Technik und Macht*. Frankfurt. [2]1978.

Newmark P., *Approaches to Translation*. Oxford. 1981.

Nida E.A., *Bible Translating. An Analysis of Principles and Procedures with Special Reference to Aboriginal Languages*. New York. 1947.

Nida E.A., *Toward a Science of Translating*. Leiden. 1964.

Nida E.A. "A Framework for the Analysis and Evaluation of Theories of Translation." In: Brislin R.W. (ed.), *Translation: Applications and Research*. New York, 47-91. 1976.

Quine M.V., "Meaning and Translation." In: Brower R.A. (ed.), *On Translation*. New York, 148-172. [2]1966.

Pinchuk I., *Scientific and Technical Translation*. London. 1977.

Popovic A., *Poetika umeleckého prekladu* (Poetics of Literary Translation). Bratislava. 1976.

Reiss K., *Texttyp und Übersetzungsmethode. Der operative Text.* Kronberg/Ts. 1976.

Roganova Z.E., *Perevod s russkogo jazyka na nemechij. Posobie po teorii perevoda (dlja institutov i fakultetov inostrannych jazykov)* (Russian-German Translation. Textbook of Translation Theory). Moscow. 1971.

Rose M.G. (ed.), *Translation Spectrum. Essays in Theory and Practice.* Albany (USA). 1981.

Soellner R., "Form und Inhalt. Betrachtungen zur literarischen und technischen Übersetzung." In: Poulsen S.-O./ Wilss W. (eds.), *Angewandte Übersetzungswissenschaft. Internationales übersetzungswissenschaftliches Kolloquium an der Wirtschaftsuniversität Aarhus/Dänemark, 19. - 21. Juni 1980.* Aarhus, 165-179. 1980.

Steiner G., *After Babel.* London. 1975.

Störig H.-J. (ed.), *Das Problem des Übersetzens.* Stuttgart. ²1969.

Vinay J.P., "Stylistique et transformation." Meta 11/1, 3-14. 1966.

Wandruszka M., *Sprachen - vergleichbar und unvergleichlich.* München. 1969.

Wandruszka M., "Kontrastive Linguistik in Österreich." In: *Anzeiger der phil.-hist. Klasse der österreichischen Akademie der Wissenschaften* 110. Wien, 1-20. 1973.

Weaver W., "Translation." In: Locke N.W./Booth A.D. (eds.), *Machine Translation of Languages.* New York, 15-23. 1955.

Weinrich H., *Linguistik der Lüge.* Heidelberg. 1966.

Wilss W., *Übersetzungswissenschaft. Probleme und Methoden.* Stuttgart. 1977.

Wilss W., "Semiotik und Übersetzungswissenschaft." In: Wilss W. (ed.), *Semiotik und Übersetzen.* Tübingen, 9-22. 1980a.

Wilss W., "Maschinelle Sprachübersetzung." In: Althaus H.P. et al. (eds.), *Lexikon der Germanistischen Linguistik.* Tübingen, 802-808. 1980b.

Wilss W., "Überlegungen zur syntaktischen Standardisierung fachsprachlicher Texte." In: Kühlwein W./Raasch A. (eds.), *Kongreßberichte der 11. Jahrestagung der Gesellschaft für Angewandte Linguistik GAL e.V., Darmstadt 1980.* Tü- bingen, 49-56. 1981a.

Wilss W., *Übersetzungswissenschaft. Ein Reader.* Darmstadt. 1981b.

Wilss W., *The Science of Translation. Problems and Methods.* Tübingen. 1982.

Zuber O. (ed.), *The Language of Theatre. Problems in the Translation and Transposition of Drama.* Oxford. 1980.

SUPPLEMENT (1982-1989)

Arntz R./Picht H., *Einführung in die übersetzungsbezogene Terminologiearbeit.* Hildesheim/Zürich/ New York. 1982.

Blatt A. et al., *Computer und Übersetzen. Eine Einführung.* Hildesheim/Zürich/New York. 1985.

Bühler H., "Textlinguistische Aspekte der Übersetzungsdidaktik." In: Wilss W./Thome G. (eds.), *Die Theorie des Übersetzens und ihr Aufschlußwert für die Übersetzungs- und Dolmetschdidaktik – Translation Theory and its Implementation in the Teaching of Translation and Interpreting.* Tübingen, 250-259. 1984.

Bühler H., "Praxisbezogene Didaktik in der Übersetzer- und Dolmetscherausbildung." *Atti del Convegno Internazionale "Tradurre: teoria ed esperienze."* Bolzano 27/2, 28/2, 1/3 1986. Bozen, 213-234. 1986.

Frank A.P., "Towards a Cultural History of Literary Translation: An Exploration of Issues and Problems in Researching the Translational Exchange between the USA and Germany." *REAL. The Yearbook of Research in English and American Literature* 4, 317-380. 1986.

Holz-Mänttäri J., *Translatorisches Handeln. Theorie und Methode.* Helsinki. 1984.

Hönig H.G., "Übersetzen zwischen Reflex und Reflexion – ein Modell der übersetzungsrelevanten Textanalyse." In: Snell-Hornby M., 230-251. 1986.

Hönig H.G./Kußmaul P., *Strategie der Übersetzung. Ein Lehr- und Arbeitsbuch.* Tübingen. 1982.

Koller W., *Einführung in die Übersetzungswissenschaft.* Heidelberg. 1979.

Königs F.G., "Der ganze Lerner soll es sein. Didaktische Überlegungen zu Aufbau und Einsatz von Übersetzungslehrbüchern." In: Königs F.G. (ed.), *Übersetzen lehren und lernen mit Büchern. Möglichkeiten und Grenzen der Erstellung und des Einsatzes von Übersetzungslehrbüchern.* Bochum, 43-63. 1987.

Krings H.P., *Was in den Köpfen von Übersetzern vorgeht. Eine empirische Untersuchung zur Struktur des Übersetzungsprozesses an fortgeschrittenen Französischlernern.* Tübingen, 1986.

Kußmaul P., "Übersetzen als Entscheidungsprozeß. Die Rolle der Fehleranalyse in der Übersetzungsdidaktik." In: Snell-Hornby M., 206-229. 1986.

Neubert A., "Übersetzen im Spannungsfeld von Wort und Text." *Parallèles* 8, 37-46. 1987

Newmark P., *A Textbook of Translation.* Hemel Hempstead. 1988.

Nida E.A./Reyburn W.D., *Meaning Across Cultures.* Maryknoll, NY. 1981.

Nida E.A./Taber C.R., *The Theory and Practice of Translation.* Leiden. 1969.

Nord C., "Zehn Thesen zum Thema 'Übersetzungslehrbuch'." In: Königs F.G. (ed.), *Übersetzen lehren und lernen mit Büchern. Möglichkeiten und Grenzen der Erstellung und des Einsatzes von Übersetzungslehrbüchern.* Bochum, 65-82. 1987.

Nord C., *Textanalyse und Übersetzen.* Heidelberg. 1988.

Reiss K. Vermeer H.J., *Grundlegung einer allgemeinen Translationstheorie.* Tübingen. 1984.

Rose M.G. (ed.), *Translation Excellence: Assessment Achievement Maintenance.* American Translators Association Scholarly Monograph Series, vol. I. Binghamton (SUNY). 1987.

Schmitz K.-D., *Automatische Segmentierung natürlichsprachlicher Sätze.* Hildesheim/Zürich/New York. 1986.

Schultze B. (ed.), *Die literarische Übersetzung. Fallstudien zu ihrer Kulturgeschichte. Göttinger Beiträge zur Internationalen Übersetzungsforschung*, vol. I. Berlin. 1987.

Snell-Hornby M. (ed.), *Übersetzungswissenschaft – eine Neuorientierung. Zur Integrierung von Theorie und Praxis*. Tübingen. 1986.

Thiel G., "Überlegungen zur übersetzungsrelevanten Textanalyse." In: Wilss W., 367-383. 1981b.

Toury G., *In Search of a Theory of Translation*. Tel Aviv. 1980.

Wilss W., "Translation Strategy, Translation Method and Translation Technique: Towards a Clarification of Three Translational Concepts." In: Université de l'Etat à Mons (ed.), *XXe anniversaire de l'Ecole d'Interprètes Internationaux. Colloque de Traductologie. Revue de Phonetique Appliquée*, 66, 67, 68, 143-152. 1983.

Wilss W., "Rhetorical and Stylistical Issues in Translation Pedagogy." *Meta* 30/3, 224-245. 1985.

Wilss W. "Zum Selbstverständnis und zum Fremdverständnis der Übersetzungswissenschaft oder: Wieviel Notiz nimmt die Öffentlichkeit von der Übersetzungswissenschaft?" In: Albrecht J. et al. (eds.), *Translation und interkulturelle Kommunikation. 40 Jahre Fachbereich Angewandte Sprachwissenschaft der Johannes-Gutenberg-Universität Mainz in Germersheim*. Frankfurt /Bern/New York/Paris, 11-25. 1987.

Wilss W., *Kognition und Übersetzen. Zu Theorie und Praxis der menschlichen und der maschinellen Übersetzung*. Tübingen. 1988a.

Wilss W., "Übersetzen als Entscheidungsprozeß." In: Arntz R. (ed.), *Textlinguistik und Fachsprache. Akten des internationalen übersetzungswissenschaftlichen AILA-Symposions in Hildesheim, 13.-16. April 1987*. Hildesheim/Zürich/New York, 7-20. 1988b.

Wilss W., "Was ist fertigkeitsorientiertes Übersetzen?" To appear. 1989a.

Wilss W., "Interferenzerscheinungen beim Übersetzen Fremdsprache-Grundsprache. Vorschläge zu einer prozeduralen Analyse." To appear. 1989b.

Das Problem des Übersetzens von Lyrik

Möglichkeiten der Kritik

Regine Knierim Solibakke
Bonn

Seit über das Übersetzen nachgedacht wird, bewegen sich Theorie und in ihrem Gefolge die übersetzerische Praxis zwischen Extrempositionen, ja beschränken sich im wesentlichen sogar auf nur zwei Gegensatzpaare, nämlich dem der "Übersetzbarkeit" bzw. "Unübersetzbarkeit" und dem des "freien" bzw. "treuen" Übersetzens. Bis etwa zur Mitte des 18. Jahrhunderts erschöpfte sich die Diskussion übersetzungstheoretischer und -praktischer Probleme in der Auseinandersetzung zwischen den beiden Grundpositionen "Freiheit" und "Treue" gegenüber dem Original. Mit der Hinwendung zum Individualismus erfuhr die Konzentration auf diese beiden Leitbegriffe dann vor allem im deutschen Kulturbereich eine grundlegende und irreversible Wandlung. Man begriff Literatur nicht mehr allein als das Wort, sondern vielmehr als ein untrennbares Zusammenwirken von Form und Inhalt, Gehalt and Gestalt, und sah in der Schöpfungskraft des Dichters ein Element, das direkt und sichtbar in die Dichtung einging. Das Übersetzen, bisher eher als Handwerk denn als literarische Tätigkeit empfunden, konnte von dieser Entdeckung des "Literarischen an sich" nicht ausgeschlossen bleiben. Die veränderte Literaturauffassung wies zwangsläufig auch die Methoden der Übersetzung von Literatur in neue Richtungen. Das Werk eines Dichters, das man jetzt,

über dessen bloße Mitteilungsfunktion hinausgehend, als kom-
plexes "sprachliches Kunstwerk" zu empfinden begann, mußte
entsprechend auch als sprachliches Kunstwerk übersetzt werden.

Die Sprach- und Literaturphilosophien ab der Mitte des 18. Jahrhunderts waren jedoch nicht nur auf die Erkenntnis und Definition
des Ästhetischen oder Literarischen an sich gerichtet. Mit der Er-
fahrung von Literatur als Sprachkunstwerk und als Resultat eines
schöpferischen Schaffensprozesses mischten sich erste Anzeichen
einer pessimistischen Sicht der Möglichkeiten von Sprache als Mittel der Verständigung. Vor allem in der Romantik sahen sich Au-
toren zum erstenmal in der Geschichte der Literatur gewissen
Grenzen des Sagbaren gegenüber; ihre Auffassung von der Inkom-
mensurabilitat des Seienden, des empfindenden Ich und des ge-
samten Universums stieß sie auf die Grenzen der Sprache. Für den
Übersetzer stellte sich somit nicht mehr die Frage zwischen Freiheit
und Treue beim Übersetzen; vielmehr mußte er fortan die viel
grundsätzlichere Frage beantworten, ob denn das sprachliche
Kunstwerk überhaupt übersetzbar sei.

"Übersetzbarkeit" impliziert allgemein ein Vertrauen in die Aus-
drucksfähigkeiten von Sprache, die es gestatte, jeden Text zu übersetzen, ohne dabei große Verluste an Gehalt oder Gestalt hinneh-
men zu müssen. Ihr Zentralbegriff ist der der "Invarianz," also der
Unveränderbarkeit des Originals. Ein Text ist demnach "übersetzbar," wenn eine das Original lückenlos und vollkommen wieder-
gebende zielsprachliche Version gefunden werden kann. Dagegen
muß jeder Text als "unübersetzbar" betrachtet werden, der auf dem
Wege der Übersetzung zu viel von seiner urprünglichen Indivi-
dualität in Form und Inhalt verliert. Im Gegensatz zu den beiden
methodologischen Termini "frei" und "treu" hat das Begriffspaar
"übersetzbar" bzw. "unübersetzbar" ästhetische und poetologische
Implikationen. Fragen der Übersetzbarkeit oder Unübersetzbarkeit
führen zu Fragen nach dem Wesen des Dichterischen im allgemeinen und nach dem Wesen des Dichterischen in einem konkret
zu übersetzenden Werk. In solchen Fragen enthüllt sich die Verbindung zwischen Übersetzung und Hermeneutik.

Unübersetzbarkeit ist bei jeder sprachlichen Übertragung ein Problem. Jeder Text, gleich ob literarischer oder nichtliterarischer Natur, enthält Sprachelemente, die zu sehr an die Eigenschaften der Ausgangssprache und an die Gesamtheit des jeweiligen Kulturraumes gebunden sind, als daß sie in die grundsätzlich anderen Gegebenheiten einer Zielsprache und ihres kulturellen Hintergrundes zu übertragen waren. Ob ein Text in seiner Gesamtheit übersetzbar ist oder nicht, hängt im wesentlichen davon ab, wie viel Unübersetzbares er enthält, d.h. wie komplex und individuell er ist. Je freier ein Ausgangstext in seiner Verwendung von Sprache, Stil und Form ist, desto leichter lassen sich Probleme der Unübersetzbarkeit von einem sprachgewandten Übersetzer lösen, desto geringer sind auch die Einbußen an Inhalt und Wirkung des Textes.

Unbestreitbar ist Lyrik die komplexeste Form von Literatur. Ihr eigentliches "Wesen" scheint geradezu darin zu bestehen, daß sie die Gesetzlichkeiten einer Sprache bis zum Äußersten auskostet und die gegebenen Elemente der Sprache zu ihrer höchsten Entfaltungs- und Ausdruckskraft führt. In großen lyrischen Kunstwerken stehen Inhalt, Sprache, Form und Expressivität gleichberechtigt nebeneinander und lassen einem Übersetzer durch ihren hohen Grad an Gesetzmäßigkeit und Strenge nur wenig Spielraum, Unübersetzbarem mit Hilfe erprobter übersetzerischer Techniken auszuweichen. Kann aber trotzdem Gottfried Benns Wort gelten: "Man kann das Gedicht als das Unübersetzbare definieren"?[1]

Prinzipiell kann jedes lyrische Werk übersetzt werden, nämlich dann, wenn sich der Übersetzer auf die Vermittlung der inhaltlichen Kategorien des Textes beschränkt und eine Prosaübersetzung liefert. Wie unzureichend und unbefriedigend ein solches Verfahren jedoch sein muß, macht Walter Benjamin im Vorwort zu seiner Übersetzung von Baudelaires Tableaux parisiens deutlich:

> Was "sagt" denn eine Dichtung? Was teilt sie denn mit? Sehr wenig dem, der sie versteht. Ihr Wesentliches ist nicht Mitteilung, nicht Aussage. Dennoch konnte diejenige Übersetzung, welche vermitteln will, nichts vermitteln als Mitteilung, also Unwesentliches. Das ist

denn auch ein Erkennungszeichen der schlechten Übersetzungen. Was aber außer der Mitteilung in einer Dichtung steht – und auch der schlechte Übersetzer gibt zu, daß es das Wesentliche ist – , gilt es nicht allgemein als das Unfaßbare, Geheimnisvolle, "Dichterische"? Das der Übersetzer nur wiedergeben kann, indem er auch dichtet? Daher rührt in der Tat ein zweites Merkmal der schlechten Übersetzung, welche man demnach als eine ungenaue Übermittlung eines unwesentlichen Inhalts definieren darf.[2]

Ein Übersetzer, der nur den Inhalt einer Dichtung überträgt und dabei für sich in Anspruch nimmt, er übersetze sie, reduziert sie damit, wie Benjamin überzeugend darstellt, auf den kleinsten Teil dessen, was ihre Qualität als sprachliches Kunstwerk ausmacht.

Wer sich als Übersetzer einem lyrischen Text nähert, muß also wissen, worin die lyrischen Qualitaten des ihm anvertrauten Werkes liegen. In keiner anderen Gattung ist aber das Problem des Gattungsspezifischen ähnlich komplex, nirgends ist man weiter von dessen Lösung entfernt als in der Lyrik. Jeder Versuch einer Gattungsdefinition der Lyrik ist schon allein wegen der historischen Vielfalt des Genres zur Unvollständigkeit, wenn nicht gar zum Scheitern verurteilt. Trotzdem soll im folgenden zumindest ein Versuch unternommen werden, die traditionellen Elemente der Lyrik darzulegen und so zu einem Begriff dessen zu kommen, was wir als "lyrisch" bezeichnen konnen.

Lyrik ist, wie alle anderen Textsorten, eine Art von Kommunikation. Ihr stehen, genau wie jenen, alle Grundelemente von Sprache zur Verfügung: Lexik, Grammatik, Syntax, Klang und Rhythmus, Vergleich und Bild, sprachliche "Register," rhetorische Figuren und andere formale Mittel. Aufgrund dieser Gemeinsamkeiten kann die Besonderheit des Lyrischen nicht – zumindest nicht nur – eine Funktion des sprachlichen Materials sein, das verwendet wird, sondern muß auf der Art und Weise beruhen, wie dieses Material, die Bauelemente der Sprache, zueinander in Verbindung gesetzt werden. Bei der Betrachtung von Lyrik durfen wir uns demnach nicht ausschließlich auf das "Was" der Sprache beschränken, sondern müssen unsere Hauptaufmerksamkeit vielmehr dem "Wie" zuwenden.

Im äußeren Aufbau liegt der am leichtesten faßbare Unterschied der Lyrik zu den anderen Literaturgattungen. Die Verwendung der Elemente Klang (als Alliteration und Assonanz, Binnen- oder Endreim, Lautmalerei u.a.), Metrum und Rhythmus ist wesentliches äußeres Merkmal für den größten Teil aller Lyrik seit dem Mittelalter. Diese ursprünglich rein formalen Elemente gewinnen im Laufe der Zeit eigenständige Aussagefunktionen. Als grundsätzlich formale Komponenten jedoch geben sie der Lyrik in der Regel den Aspekt der Formstrenge, des Strukturierten, bisweilen sogar der Formenge; Lyrik ist diejenige literarische Darbietungsform, in welcher der formale Aspekt von zentraler Bedeutung ist als in Epik oder Drama. Die lyrische Dichtung ist am stärksten und häufigsten der Begrenzung durch Metrum, Kolon, Zeile, Strophe, Reim oder gar, wie beim Sonett, durch eine vorgeschriebene Länge unterworfen. In der Tat sind relative Kürze und Prägnanz, Funktionen der Formstrenge, die einzigen gattungsspezifischen Kennzeichen der Lyrik.[3] Die formalen Begrenzungen haben direkt Einfluß auf alle anderen Aspekte des lyrischen Sprechens, da sie den Dichter dazu zwingen, das gedankliche Material in besonderen sprachlichen Formen darzustellen. Sie zwingen zu besonders kunstvoller oder gar virtuoser Verwendung der jeweils verfügbaren Sprache und sind der Hauptgrund, weshalb die Sprache der Lyrik vor allen anderen literarischen Ausdrucksformen zu einem besonders hohen Grad an Abstrahierung, Stilisierung, Verschlüsselung und Sprachschöpfung neigt.

Über die inhaltliche Struktur wurde bereits gesprochen. Obwohl Benjamins Ausführungen über den eher sekundären Charakter der Mitteilung in einer lyrischen Dichtung unmittelbar überzeugen, darf die Mitteilungsfunktion des Gedichts doch nicht vollkommen vernachlässigt werden. Vor allem jene lyrischen Werke, die sich um die dichterische Darstellung philosophischer Inhalte bemühen, machen dies deutlich. Wir müssen uns hier auf den Begriff der Invarianz zurückbesinnen. Wie bei jeder anderen Übersetzung lautet auch bei der Übersetzung von Lyrik die Forderung an den Übersetzer, den Aussagegehalt unverfälscht in die zielsprachliche Version zu übertragen. So eindeutig und einsichtig diese Forderung aber auch ist, so schwierig ist sie gerade bei Lyrik zu erfüllen. Denn wenn auch der rein sachlichen Information in der Lyrik in der Regel nur sekundäre Bedeutung zukommt, so besteht doch das "Wesen" dieser Gattung gerade darin, wie diese Mitteilung sprachkünstlerisch ausgestaltet wird. Es erweist sich, daß der Lyrikübersetzer – genauso wie übrigens sein Kritiker – unmöglich das "Was" des Gedichts vom "Wie" trennen kann, ohne damit das Wesen, das Eigentliche des Lyrischen zu verletzen und aufzubrechen: das enge Verwobensein von Gehalt und Gestalt. In ihm liegt die Expressivität von Lyrik. An der sprachlichen Ausformung, an der "Sprachgewalt" zeigen sich die Meisterschaft des Dichters und die Größe seines Werkes, und sie müssen vom Übersetzer erfaßt und in ihrer Eigenart angestrebt werden.

Die Sprache der Lyrik will im traditionellen Gedicht über die Normalsprache und selbst über die Sprache der anderen literarischen Gattungen hinausgehen. Gehobene sprachliche Form allein ist zwar noch kein spezifisches Gattungsmerkmal der Lyrik, da sie sich auch in der Prosa von Epik und Dramatik und natürlich im Versdrama findet; aber der lyrische Dichter arbeitet bewußter und konzentrierter mit seiner Sprache, da ihn die Begrenztheit der Form zu besonders hoher Dichte und Gespanntheit zwingt. Wie in keiner anderen Gattung wird der Dichter von Lyrik so zur äußersten Ausschöpfung von Sprache getrieben. Sprachschöpfung ist das eigentliche Geheimnis und das Wesen der Lyrik. Sprachschöpfung ist Abweichung von der Normalsprache, aber auch Abweichung von der bewußten Sprache der anderen literarischen Darbietungsformen. Sprachschöpfung ist die neuartige, oft be- oder verfremdende Verknüpfung des zu einem geschichtlichen Zeitpunkt verfügbaren Sprachmaterials zu neuen Wortkombinationen, neuen, ausdrucksstärkeren Metaphern, Bildern und Symbolen, die Erforschung und Ausschöpfung des Klangreichtums der Sprache und ihres Rhythmus, die Verdichtung, Abstrahierung oder Stilisierung der Sprache. Sprachschöpfung ist ein uneingeschränkt subjektiver Vorgang, ausgelost und gesteuert von dem Bedürfnis und dem

Willen des Dichters, etwas auf eine unwiderrufliche und unnach-
ahmbare Art und Weise zu sagen. Ihm kommt es nicht darauf an,
etwas per se Neues zu sagen, sondern darauf, daß er das, was er
zu sagen hat, neu sagt. Es soll für die lyrische Dichtung kein
Präzedens geben, – wie kann es da eines für die Übersetzung
geben?

Die sprachschöpferische Qualität des lyrischen Kunstwerkes
wird damit zum Hauptproblem und zum Hauptprüfstein für den
Übersetzer. Bevor er überhaupt beginnen kann zu übersetzen, muß
er die sprachliche Eigenart und Einmaligkeit seiner Vorlage zu
erfassen suchen. Dabei muß ihm dieselbe Freiheit des Interpre-
tierens zugestanden werden, die jedem individuellen Leser und
jedem literaturwissenschaftlich Analysierenden eingeräumt wird.
Seine Aufgabe ist es dann, das Ergebnis seiner Beschäftigung mit
dem Originalkunstwerk dichterisch zu formulieren – genauso wie
der individuelle Leser oder der Literaturwissenschaftler sein eigenes Verstehen durch die ihm zur Verfügung stehende Sprache und
die ihm zugrunde liegende Erfahrenswelt ausdrückt. Der laien-
hafte Leser und der Literaturwissenschaftler werden sich dabei der
Normalsprache, möglicherweise einer gehobenen Normalsprache
oder eines wissenschaftlichen Jargons bedienen. Sie werden ana-
lysieren und paraphrasieren, auslegen und explizit deuten. Der
dichterische Übersetzer aber wird versuchen, dem Dichter des
Originals auf seinem sprachschöpferischen Wege zu folgen. Seine
Analyse und seine Paraphrasierung, seine inhaltliche und formale
Deutung gehen in seine Übersetzung ein, sind implizit in ihr enthalten. Wie das fremdsprachliche Vorbild wird er sich an die Begrenzung der Form halten und sich der Norm des Originalkunst-
werkes unterwerfen. Wo in der ursprünglichen Dichtung Spracher-
neuerung aufgrund innerer, subjektiver Impulse oder Zwänge er-
folgt, findet sie in der Übersetzung aufgrund der äußeren Impulse
oder Zwänge statt, die in der Autorität des Originals begründet
liegen. Genauso wie sich der Dichter des Originals in sprachliches
Neuland vorwagt, muß sich auch der ihm verpflichtete Übersetzer
um "Urbarmachung sprachlichen Brachlandes" (Franz Rosen-

zweig)[4] bemühen. Dabei kann es sich nicht um den Versuch einer Imitation mit dem Ziel der restlosen Deckungsgleichheit des sprachlichen Ausdrucks handeln. Was aber möglich ist und daher von dem Übersetzer gefordert werden muß, ist größtmögliche Annäherung an das, worin das Einmalige und Expressive des fremden Dichtwerkes besteht. Er muß versuchen, das Zusammenwirken aller verschiedenen Strukturen der Dichtung und die nur subjektiv erfaßbare, poetologisch und literaturwissenschaftlich kaum eindeutig definierbare "Lyrizität" zu erfassen.

In der Tat wird ihn dieses Bemühen an die Grenzen der Übersetzbarkeit führen, die er aber durch den Mut zu eigener Sprachschöpfung – gemäß der Norm, die ihm das Original aufzwingt, – erweitern kann. Der Übersetzer muß die Herausforderung annehmen, die ihm der Dichter des Originals entgegenhält. Er muß das Dichtwerk als Provokation empfinden, seine eigenen Fähigkeiten des Verstehens und dichterischen Nachvollziehens voll auszuschreiten und anhand eines großen Vorbildes oder Lehrmeisters zu erweitern. Oft wird er die Grenzen seines Tuns einsehen und verzichten müssen, sei es, weil seine Sprache als solche nicht flexibel oder erneuerbar genug ist, oder sei es, weil seine persönlichen sprachschöpferischen Fähigkeiten begrenzt sind. Andererseits kann sich ihm aber auch die Möglichkeit bieten, in seiner Sprache das Original durch Größeres zu übertreffen. Verlust und Ersatz stehen in der Übertragung von Lyrik eng beieinander. Sie müssen sich die Waage halten und sind gewiß die wichtigsten Kriterien für eine Kritik: Geht zu viel verloren, so ist das Bemühen umsonst gewesen und hätte nie unternommen werden sollen; zu viel Ersatz deutet entweder auf eine minderwertige Originaldichtung oder auf zu wenig Respekt des Übersetzers vor dem Original. Was dann vorliegt, ist eine freie Bearbeitung eines Urtextes, die ohne weiteres als eigenständiges Werk und isoliert von der Vorlage zu werten ist.

Für die wissenschaftlich-technische Übersetzung wurde eine prinzipielle Übersetzbarkeit vorausgesetzt. Kann dies nach dem Gesagten auch für die Übersetzung von Lyrik gelten? Die Übersetzung oder sprachliche Nachgestaltung läßt sich nicht vom Ver-

stehen des Originals trennen: Ist dieser Text grundsätzlich versteh-
bar, also nachvollziehbar, so ist auch der dichterische Nachvollzug
grundsätzlich möglich, wenn sich ein Vermittler seiner annimmt,
der über seine Sprache in ähnlicher Weise verfügt wie sein Vorbild.
Hier, wo die Frage der Übersetzbarkeit mit Problemen des Verstehens, mit Fragen der Hermeneutik, zusammentrifft, offenbart
sich die falsche Prämisse, auf der die Forderung nach der "voll-
kommenen" Übersetzung beruht, die in dem Begriff der Übersetzbarkeit impliziert ist. Die vollkommene Übersetzung würde
das vollkommene, lückenlose Verstehen einer Dichtung vorausset-
zen. Gerade das aber ist nicht möglich, ja nicht einmal wünschens-
wert. Keine Dichtung ist jemals "fertig" in dem Sinn, daß sie auf
einen von jedem Leser oder Interpreten jederzeit nachvollzieh-
baren Nenner gebracht werden konnte. Jeder, der original schaf-
fend tätig ist, strebt ein Ideal an, das aber im individuellen Kunstwerk nur unvollkommen erreicht ist. Genauso aber wie ein eigenständiges Kunstwerk nur eine Stufe im dynamischen Prozeß des
Gesamtschaffens eines Dichters sein kann, wird auch dessen Verständnis und Wirken nie abgeschlossen, nie "vollkommen" sein.

Eine Übersetzung oder Nachdichtung ist nur ein Baustein zum
Verstehen eines Textes. In ihr tut der Übersetzer in der ihm ge-
mäßen Weise dasselbe, was jeder Leser und jeder Literaturwissenschaftler, ja selbst der Dichter selbst tut: Er bietet seine Version,
sein Verstehen und seine Auseinandersetzung mit dem Ideal an
und trägt damit zum Fortwirken und Fortleben eines Werkes und
seines Dichters bei. Das Ziel selbst, das "Vollkommene" jemals zu
erreichen, ist eine fruchtbare und wohl unabdingbar notwendige
Illusion.

Darin liegen der Sinn und die Daseinsberechtigung der Lyrik-
übersetzung. Darin liegen aber auch die Schwierigkeiten jeder Kritik. Denn wenn eine Übersetzung Resultat der subjektiven Sicht
der Übersetzers ist, in das seine eigene Subjektivität und Sprachgewalt einfließen, wie kann dann eine ihrerseits von subjektivem
Werkverständnis ausgehende Kritik objektiv werten? Die Frage
kann nicht abschließend beantwortet werden. Sie ist in noch un-

gelöste Probleme der literarischen Wertung und Wertbarkeit ein-
gebettet. Was immer an Kategorien für die Beurteilung einer Übersetzung aufgestellt werden mag, unterliegt der Subjektivität des
Kritikers, ganz abgesehen davon, daß eindeutige und allgemein
anerkannte Kriterien für die literarische Wertung eines Textes nicht
existieren. Mit diesem Vorbehalt soll als eine mögliche Kategorie
für die Übersetzungskritik der Begriff "Texttreue" vorgeschlagen
werden, so wie ihn die moderne Übersetzungstheorie definiert.
Der Begriff hat nichts mit sklavischem Kleben am Wort oder an der
grammatischen und sprachlichen Form des Originals gemein.
Höchstes Ziel einer "texttreuen" literarischen Übersetzung ist vielmehr eine "allseitige Treue zum Textganzen."[5] Diese Formulierung
Georges Mounins deutet die traditionell erstickend enggefaßte Definition der Texttreue in ähnlich offener Weise um wie die neue
Konzeption der "Wörtlichkeit" bei Wolfgang Schadewaldt, der darin "die große, alles durchdringende Verpflichtung dem Wort des
Dichters und seiner Wahrheit gegenüber"[6] sieht. Der Übersetzer,
inspiriert von der Einmaligkeit des Originals, will sich ihm auf
seine Weise nähern und – in scheinbarer Paradoxie – das, was er
als unerreichbar und unwiederholbar erkannt hat, erreichen und
wiederholen. Er weiß, daß er bestenfalls etwas "Wesensgleiches"
(Wolfgang Schadewaldt) schaffen kann, und darauf muß sich sein
ganzes Bemühen richten. Das Kriterium der "Wesensgleichheit"
oder "Wesensähnlichkeit," das sowohl in Mounins als auch in
Schadewaldts Deutungen der verwandten Begriffe "Textreue" und
"Wörtlichkeit" enthalten ist, scheint sich dem Kritiker als einziger,
zugegebenermaßen unscharfer Bewertungsmaßstab anzubieten.

   In diesem Begriff der "Treue" zum Original lösen sich die Grundprobleme des Übersetzens von Lyrik zu einer vorläufigen Antwort
auf: Die Frage "übersetzbar oder nicht" wird unerheblich, da ihre
falsche Prämisse, die Forderung nach Imitation, offenbar ist. Das
Nachdenken über das eigentliche Wesen der Lyrik deutet in eine
ganz andere Richtung: Eine Dichtung kann und soll nicht ganz
erfaßbar und damit auch nicht ganz übersetzbar sein, wenn sie
über ihre Zeit hinaus Gültigkeit behalten will. "Der Prozeß (des

Übersetzens) wird wichtiger als das Ziel; der Weg wird zum Ziel. Es ist schon ein Fehler zu sagen, das Ziel sei nicht erreichbar, weil es zu erreichen gar nicht denkbar ist. Die Unerreichbarkeit des Zieles ist seine Vollendung. Eben dies ist der gemeinsame Ursprung des Dichtens, Verstehens und Übersetzens."[7]

Im folgenden werden einige Erkenntnisse aus der vorangegangenen theoretischen Diskussion anhand von fünf Übersetzungen von Rainer Maria Rilkes Gedicht "Der Panther" in die Praxis umgesetzt.[8] Dabei wird kein Anspruch auf eine umfassende Übersetzungskritik erhoben. Es sollen vielmehr Anregungen zu einer Auseinandersetzung des Lesers mit den vorgestellten Texten (siehe Anhang) gegeben werden. Die Auswahl der fünf Versionen aus einer schier unüberschaubaren Anzahl von Übersetzungen wurde einerseits von der Frage bestimmt, ob und wie sich die Herme-. neutik des Übersetzens in der konkreten Übersetzungsarbeit niederschlage. Ein Vergleich zwischen verschiedenen Fassungen eines und desselben Übersetzers bot sich hier an. Eine gewisse Neugier und der Reiz des Gegensätzlichen waren dann Gründe für die zusätzliche Gegenüberstellung verschiedener Übersetzer: Wie würden zwei von Herkunft und persönlichem Interesse so verschieden motivierte Übersetzer an Rilkes Werk herangehen?

"Der Panther" entstand unter dem Einfluß von Rilkes Berührung mit Auguste Rodin, dessen bildhauerisches Schaffen dem jungen Lyriker die für sein neues künstlerisches Konzept des Dinggedichts entscheidenden Impulse verlieh. Rodin wurde zu Rilkes Lehrmeister, der forderte, daß auch der Dichter, ganz wie der bildende Künstler, vor jede künstlerische Ausgestaltung eines Gegenstandes oder Lebewesens dessen vertiefte Beobachtung stelle. Allein die verinnerlichende Anschauung eines Objektes setze den Künstler instand, zu dessen wesenhaftem Kern vorzudringen, und erst die Erkenntnis des Wesenhaften der Dinge erlaube deren Umformung ins Künstlerische. Unter dem Eindruck von Rodins Maxime "Il faut toujours travailler – toujours – "[9] begann Rilke, sich in seinem lyrischen Schaffen zu strenger Arbeit am Objekt und an der sprachlichen Gestaltung zu erziehen. Alles Willkürliche und Überflüssige sollte aus seinem Schreiben verbannt werden. Damit strebte er das an, was ihn an Rodins Werk so faszinierte: die Sublimation des "Dings" zum "Kunstding."[10] Die *Neuen Gedichte* (1903), zu denen "Der Panther" zählt, sind erstes Resultat dieser Arbeit. Klassischer Aufbau und starker Formwille sind eines ihrer hervorragenden gemeinsamen Merkmale. Rilkes neue Ästhetik des Objektivismus, der reinen Anschauung und künstlerischen Selbstdisziplin führt ihn zu einem lyrischen Stil, in dem sich alle sprachlichen und formalen Elemente mit der philosophischen Idee zu einem Kunstwerk von eindrucksvoller Dichte und Ausdruckskraft verbinden. Seine neuen literarästhetischen Prinzipien erlangen daher auch für den Prozeß der Analyse, des Verstehens und Übersetzens der Dinggedichte zentrale Bedeutung.

Innerhalb eines Jahres veröffentlichte der zeitgenössische nordamerikanische Dichter Robert Bly zwei Übersetzungen von "Der Panther." Wie seine begleitenden Kommentare zu Rilkes Dinggedicht zeigen, steht die Ästhetik der reinen Anschauung im Mittelpunkt des Interesses, das Bly als Dichter-Übersetzer dem Werk Rilkes entgegenbringt. Er unterstreicht wiederholt die zentrale Bedeutung, die dem Akt des gesammelten Sehens, "concentrated seeing,"[11] im schöpferischen Prozeß des Dinggedichts zukomme. Blys Übersetzungen dokumentieren jedoch, daß sein Versuch, den schöpferischen Akt nachzuvollziehen, an eben diesem Punkt stehenbleibt. Der zweite, für Rilkes Dichten entscheidende Schritt, die künstlerische Umformung des Beobachteten durch strukturierende Formgebung, ist in Blys Übersetzungen nicht wiederzufinden. Im Gegenteil: Der Übersetzer wird durch seine persönliche Fixierung dazu verleitet, die von Rilke in den ersten beiden Zeilen dargestellte Bewegung als "seeing" zu reproduzieren. Um die Synonym- und Klangwiederholungen des Originals zu übersetzen, wiederholt er dieses Wort sogar viermal. In dieser Übersetzung gehen die wesentlichen Elemente von Rilkes Darstellung verloren: das rastlose Auf- und Abgehen des gefangenen Tieres und das seine Sinne lähmende Vorbeigleiten der Gitterstäbe, das jeden Blick auf die Welt draußen verzerrt. Blys schwerstes Versäumnis in seiner ersten

Version liegt aber darin, daß er weder den Panther noch die Stäbe des Käfigs überhaupt mit einem Wort erwähnt und so das eigentliche Objekt des von ihm so sehr bewunderten objektorientierten Sehens ganzlich außer acht läßt. Offenbar erkannte Bly dann später, daß seine erste Übersetzung das Original verfehlt hatte, und bemühte sich in seinem zweiten Versuch um eine adäquatere Wiedergabe, die ihm im Ansatz auch gelingt. Aber auch dem Leser der revidierten Fassung bleibt das Moment der schon automatenhaften Bewegung des Tieres weiterhin verborgen.

In keiner seiner beiden Übersetzungen fängt Bly das für das Originalgedicht so charakteristische kontinuierliche Fließen der Sprache, des Metrums und des Rhythmus ein. Überhaupt scheinen ihn die Formgesetze des Rilkeschen Dinggedichts wenig zu interessieren. So leiden beide Übersetzungen unter einer im Vergleich zum Original geradezu frappierenden Formlosigkeit. Ohne die für die Gesamtaussage so wichtige Kontrolle über Klang, Metrum und Rhythmus und ohne das strukturierende Reimschema bleibt dem englischsprachigen Leser der Zugang zu "Der Panther" verschlossen. Beiden Übersetzungen Blys fehlt trotz einiger treffender Formulierungen (I, 3-4 und III, 1-2 in beiden Versionen) die Wirkung des Originals, da die Verschmelzung von Gehalt und Gestalt nicht erreicht wird. Blys Scheitern erwächst in erster Linie aus einem unzureichenden Verständnis und Nachvollzug der ästhetischen Prinzipien des Dinggedichts.

Anders als Robert Bly versteht sich James B. Leishman nicht als übersetzender Dichter, sondern als Sprach- und Literaturforscher, für den die Übersetzung ein Mittel zum Verständnis eines Werkes sein kann. So schreibt er im Vorwort zu einer seiner englischen Rilke-Ausgaben, seine jahrzehntelange Übersetzertätigkeit sei "not only a matter of finding a more adequate, or less inadequate, expression for something which I think I have completely understood; it is sometimes a matter of coming to understand, or thinking that I have come to understand, the original for the first time."[12] Leishmans drei Übersetzungen, entstanden 1949, 1957 und 1959, belegen den hermeneutisch fundierten Ansatz dieses Übersetzers.

Gerade die beiden ersten Zeilen von Rilkes Gedicht, die absichtlich den Bezugspunkt offenlassen und so die Auflösung symbolisieren, der die in Naturgesetzen festgefügte Welt des Panthers zum Opfer fällt, stellen durch ihre raffinierte sprachliche Ambiguitat eine schwere Herausforderung an den übersetzenden Interpreten. Während im Deutschen die Formulierung "Vorübergehn der Stäbe" sowohl als Objekt- als auch als Subjektgenitiv ausgelegt werden und entsprechend verschiedene Bedeutungen annehmen kann, zwingen die grammatischen Gesetze der englischen Sprache den Übersetzer zu einer klaren Entscheidung für die eine oder die andere Perspektive. Leishman experimentiert in seinen drei Übersetzungen mit beiden Ausdeutungen. Er kommt in der Version von 1957 Rilkes doppeldeutiger Formulierung sogar recht nahe. Auch aus formalen Grunden ist dieser Fassung des Gedichtanfangs der Vorzug vor den beiden anderen Übersetzungen zu geben. Deutlich ist das Bemühen des Übersetzers zu spüren, das Ungleichgewicht zwischen der in seiner ersten Version noch fehlenden metrischen Struktur und dem zumindest partiell gelösten Problem des Reimschemas zu beheben. Die mittlere Fassung bringt diese Formprobleme einer akzeptablen Lösung näher. In seiner letzten Übersetzung hebt Leishman das zuvor Erreichte durch unnötiges Verlängern und Aufsplittern der ersten Zeile aber fast völlig wieder auf.

Leishmans Übersetzungen offenbaren ein tieferes Verständnis der Ästhetik des Dinggedichts als Blys. Die Korrekturen, die der Autor vor allem zwischen der ersten und der zweiten Version eingefügt hat, belegen deutlich seine Suche nach einer Formulierung, die dem englischsprachigen Leser Rilkes Prinzip der lyrischen Klarheit und sprachlich-gedanklichen Ökonomie vermitteln soll. Im Gegensatz zu Robert Bly ist sich James Leishman stets der außerordentlichen Bedeutung des formalen Elementes für die Wirkung des Dinggedichts bewußt. Seine Übersetzungen sind daher auch trotz mancher sprachlicher Ungeschicklichkeiten unter dem Kriterium der "Wesensgleichheit" als gelungener zu bezeichnen als die seines Übersetzerkollegen.

Die hier ausgesprochene Kritik an den fünf zur Diskussion ge-
stellten Übersetzungen konzentriert sich auf den Teilaspekt des
Formalen und Literarästhetischen. Eine detaillierte sprachliche
Übersetzungskritik erscheint, auch im vorgegebenen Rahmen, eher
sekundär. Gerade am Beispiel von "Der Panther" erweist sich, daß
auch die beste Einzelformulierung, daß rein sprachliches Gelingen
das Scheitern des Übersetzers an den konzeptionellen und struk-
turellen Anforderungen seiner Vorlage nicht wettmachen können.
Zudem läßt sich der Verdacht nicht ganz von der Hand weisen, daß
Bly die Bedeutung des Gesagten nicht immer ganz erfaßt, wie die
"schiefen" Übertragungen von II, 2 und III, 3 zeigen. Hier ist nicht
einmal die Grundforderung der Invarianz erfüllt.

Leishmans Arbeit verdient aufgrund derselben Überlegungen
den Vorrang, wobei die mittlere Fassung des Gedichts die Probleme des Übersetzens wohl am besten löst. Aber auch bei Leishman
wird deutlich, daß gerade die Struktur des Dinggedichts den Übersetzer vor nahezu unlösbare Aufgaben stellt. Trotz eines hohen
Grades an analytischer Durchdringung des Originals erreichen
auch Leishmans Übersetzungen nicht das Ziel allen Übersetzens,
den Anspruch des Werkes unvermindert zu vermitteln.

Ungeachtet aller Kritik darf nicht vergessen werden, daß Bly und
Leishman eine große Herausforderung angenommen haben. Sie
haben es unternommen, das Wesenhafte eines Gedichts aufzu-
spüren und nachzuvollziehen, das seinen Interpreten noch immer
Stoff zur Auseinandersetzung gibt. Gerade dadurch erweist "Der
Panther" seine Größe als Kunstwerk. So bestätigen Leishman und
Bly und mit ihnen die vielen anderen Übersetzer dieses Gedichts
ungewollt den Aphorismus Jean Pauls: "Ein Wunderwerk, das
einer Übersetzung fähig ist, ist keiner wert."

ANMERKUNGEN

1. Gottfried Benn, *Gesammelte Werke*. 4 Bde., hgg. v. Dieter Wellershoff (Wiesbaden: Limes Verlag, 1959 u.o.). Bd. 1, S. 510.

2. Hans J. Störig, Hrsg., *Das Problem des Übersetzens*. Wege der Forschung, Bd. VIII (Darmstadt: Wissenschaftliche Buchgesellschaft, 1963). S. 182-83.

3. Bernhard Asmuth, *Aspekte der Lyrik*, 5., erw. Aufl. (Opladen: Westdeutscher Verlag, 1979). S. 129.

4. Zit. n. Rolf Kloepfer, *Die Theorie der literarischen Übersetzung* (München: W. Fink Verlag, 1967). S. 76.

5. Georges Mounin, *Die Übersetzung; Geschichte, Theorie, Anwendung* (München: Nymphenburger Verlagsbuchhandlung, 1967). S. 118.

6. Zit. n. Kloepfer, S. 73.

7. Zit. n. Kloepfer, S. 123.

8. Das Originalgedicht und die hier diskutierten Übersetzungen finden sich im Anhang, s.u.

9. *Rainer Maria Rilke/Lou Andreas-Salome: Briefwechsel*, hgg. v. Ernst Pfeiffer (Frankfurt: Insel Verlag, 1975). S. 103.

10. ebd., S. 94.

11. Robert Bly, Übers., *Selected Poems of Rainer Maria Rilke* (New York: Harper & Row, 1980), S. 133-37; R. Bly, Hrsg., *News of the Universe* (San Francisco: Sierra Club Books, 1981), S. 210-12.

12. James B. Leishman, Übers., *Rainer Maria Rilke: Selected Works*. Vol II, *Poetry* (London: Hogarth Press, 1967). S. 22.

Anhang

DER PANTHER
Im Jardin des plantes, Paris

Sein Blick ist vom Vorübergehn der Stäbe
so müd geworden, daß er nichts mehr hält.
Ihm ist, als ob es tausend Stäbe gäbe
und hinter tausend Stäben keine Welt.

Der weiche Gang geschmeidig starker Schritte,
der sich im allerkleinsten Kreise dreht,
ist wie ein Tanz von Kraft um eine Mitte,
in der betäubt ein großer Wille steht.

Nur manchmal schiebt der Vorhang der Pupille
sich lautlos auf – . Dann geht ein Bild hinein,
geht durch der Glieder angespannte Stille –
und hört im Herzen auf zu sein.

(R.M. Rilke, *Gesammelte Gedichte*, S. 261)

* * *

Robert Bly:

THE PANTHER
Jardin des Plantes, Paris

From seeing and seeing the seeing has become so exhausted
it no longer sees anything anymore.
The world is made of bars, a hundred thousand
bars, and behind the bars, nothing.

The lithe swinging of that rhythmical easy stride
that slowly circles down to a single point
is like a dance of energy around a hub,
in which a great will stands stunned and numb.

At times the curtains of the eye lift
without a sound – then a shape enters,
slips through the tightened silence of the shoulders,
reaches the heart and dies.

(*News of the Universe*, 247)

THE PANTHER
In the Jardin des Plantes, Paris

From seeing the bars, his seeing is so exhausted
that it no longer holds anything anymore.
To him the world is bars, a hundred thousand bars,
and behind the bars, nothing.

The lithe swinging of that rhythmical easy stride
which circles down to the tiniest hub
is like a dance of energy around a point
in which a great will stands stunned and numb.

Only at times the curtains of the pupil rise
without a sound . . . then a shape enters,
slips through the tightened silence of the shoulders,
reaches the heart, and dies.

(*Selected Poems*, 139)

James B. Leishman:

THE PANTHER
Jardin des Plantes, Paris

His glance, so tired from traversing his cage's
repeated railings, can hold nothing more.
He feels as though there were a thousand cages
and no more world thereafter than before.

The padding of the strong and supple pace,
within the tiniest circle circumscribed,
is like a dance of force about a basis
on which a mightly will stands stupefied.

And only now and then a noiseless lifting
of the eye's curtain, till an image dart,
go through the limbs' intensive silence drifting –
and cease for ever in the heart.   (*R.M. Rilke, Requiem*, 91)

THE PANTHER
Jardin des Plantes, Paris

His gaze, those bars keep passing, is so misted
with tiredness, it can take in nothing more.
He feels as though a thousand bars existed,
and no more world beyond them than before.

Those supple-powerful paddings, turning there
in tiniest of circles, well might be
the dance of forces round a center where
some mighty will stands paralyticly.

Just now and then the pupil's noiseless shutter
is lifted. – Then an image will indart,
down through the limbs' intensive stillness flutter
and end its being in the heart.

(Possibilities of Being, 91)

THE PANTHER
Jardin des Plantes, Paris

His gaze, going past those bars, has got so misted
with tiredness, it can take in nothing more.
He feels as though a thousand bars existed,
and no more world beyond them than before.

Those supple powerful paddings, turning there
in tiniest of circles, well might be
the dance of forces round a centre where
some mighty will stands paralyticly.

Just now and then the pupil's noiseless shutter
is lifted. – Then an image will indart,
down through the limbs' intensive stillness flutter
and end its being in the heart.

(R.M. Rilke: Selected Works, II, 78)

Reflections on the Limits of Translatability

Paul Celan in English

Richard Exner
University of California, Santa Barbara

The degree of sophistication to which the theory of translation has risen in these post-structuralist and semiotic days, and the amount of material published on the subject of translation *After Babel* and, lastly, the degree of sophistication of nearly all the texts of the late Rilke and the late Celan and of at least some of the commentaries on these texts, written or, in some cases, inspired by such figures as Gadamer, Szondi, Benjamin and Derrida.

All this seems to make us look foolish if we start another round of argument on the question of untranslatability. Today we are aware of inter-lingual transpositions of communicable signs, silences and mutenesses as well as of "atmospheric" elements in translation, and so may find it perhaps much more difficult to translate a non-hermetic poem by Eichendorff which carries an easy message than a post-Mallarmé poem in which language and syntax have become, quite literally, particularized and have thereby alone become translatable again, particle by particle. "Atmospheric" means, I think, also a tradition within which one translates. The knowledge of George Herbert's and John Donne's language, for example, will stand a translator of Gryphius and Spee in good stead indeed. I also consider it impossible to do justice in English (or in any other language for that matter) to the poetry of the middle and late Celan without having first mastered the problems which arise from translating the Rilke of the *Neue Gedichte* and a later period:

> The style of Celan's poetry is based on the poetry of Rilke. That means that if you should attempt to translate the poetry of Celan you should first have a solid grounding in the translation of poetry by Rainer Maria Rilke.

I wish to take George Steiner's four steps of translation from the beginning of this chapter on "The Hermeneutic Motion," namely trust, aggression, incorporation, and reciprocity as proven and by now self-evident, just as self-evident as his amply illustrated point of "understanding as translation" in an earlier chapter of the same *After Babel*. We should, at the outset, understand that "understanding as translation" must be extended to the act of writing, that the writing and making real of a poem *is an act of translating certain imaginative and intellectual processes of the mind* into words or into verbal, more exactly, grammatical or syntactical sign units. These processes need not necessarily be made *palatable* by the translator in the host or target language; rather, the host or target language should be advanced *toward* the text in question until it ap- proximates it to a point of indistinguishability. Any cost to the target language, in terms of easy and customary accessibility, really does not matter. For example, rather than giving a hint (or more than a hint) of Celan or the late Rilke in perfectly normal and understandable English, we should move English *toward* Rilke or Celan, Rilke-ize, Celan-ize English even at the risk of straining the limits of understandability. One instance must suffice: I believe that Celan's "entimmern" delivers the same alienating and connotative shock in German as does "to dis-ever" in English; only (at least) bi-lingual readers can judge to what degree the later Hölderlin or the late Rilke or Paul Celan with *Atemwende* and after have become strange and alien to the native ear. And *if* alien, why should the texts sound more "normal" to the ear of the reader of the transla- tion? Difficult, probably; hermetic, perhaps; hard to intepret, pos- sibly; text and translation however must give reader and listener that certain shock and shudder which comes when language has *moved*, suddenly, repeatedly, by infinitesimal, barely observable, vibration or by a rude shock or roll — I chose seismic references deliberately. Poets have often spoken of themselves as seismographic instruments. On the other hand: Re-creating linguistic effects or verbal nonsense which is to mask the non-sense of language is good practice for a translater, good challenge, and good fun. But rilke-izing or celan-izing or creating an English Mallarmé or an English Stefan George is something quite different. As translators we must, I repeat, transpose mental processes which, in the case of Celan, might confront us with a language, already fully translated, particularly in Celan's case. I agree with George Steiner's argument, set forth in connection with Celan's own translations, that by way of translating, Celan had been able to "displace German," a language with which he "coexisted self-destructively" into "a position of salutary strangeness. He could approach it with therapeutic dispassion as a raw material fatally his own yet also contingent and potentially hostile." "All of Celan's poetry," Steiner summarizes, "is translated *into* German. In the process, the receptor-language becomes un-housed, broken, idio-syncratic almost to the point of non-communication." To the point, I wish to add, of untranslatability. "It becomes," Steiner again, "a meta-German cleansed of historical-political dirt and, thus alone, usable by a profoundly Jewish voice after the Holocaust." Steiner thinks that we cannot and must not separate Celan's efforts at translation from the rest of his work. I would go a step further, in two directions, and say: First, translating for Celan had very early become an act of *remembrance*. Celan, by translating Shakespeare for example, seems to yearn for a time and mental process in which language was not yet contaminated, neither at the source nor at the target. Remembrance, then, being a setting-free from one's own time and fate, almost serves as a kind of depersonalization. And secondly, anticipating my later arguments on muteness and the virtual cancellation of writing by writing, I would suggest that Celan consciously as well as subconsciously, destructs language, specifically the German language, destructs it out of its customary existence into "Unlesbarkeit" — an "intelligibility" in the full sense of the word: communication has ceased; there is nothing left to read.

Celan, then, does not simply create neologisms, *hapax legomena* or phonic/visual manipulations; rather, he operates with lexical and phonetic events that are intimately tied to and continually spring from the very sources of this meta-language, i.e., from highly complex mental and emotional processes. Language, German in this instance, ceases to be, if communication (in German) has ceased to be, if tenuous human-shaped communication has ceased to be.

Celan did not spare his own early work. It can for example be argued that Celan, in the poem "Weggebeizt," refers to "das Mein-Gedicht," i.e., his own earlier poetry, along with conventional metaphoric poetry in general. Convention, even in the form of poetically reshaped discourse, ceased to be usable or communicable to Celan once the enormity of the historical events which had, after all, occurred also in language, had impressed themselves upon him. Celan of course was a *modern* poet, aware of the disturbed or ruptured interconnections within the famous triad of reader, poet, and text. It should not surprise us as translators, then, if we often confront texts in Celan whose *words* are perfectly translatable but whose *condition* and *message* is not.

The area of principal concern and worry is therefore not with vocabulary or reference and allusion, but with the externalization of an author's internal creative processes. The lesser translator's job, Stefan George had once remarked, is to research and adequately re-create an author's linguistic fall-out, as it were: sentences, images, concepts, prosodic detail and specialized vocabulary, ichthyological, botanical, or whatever — *instructable* things, in other words. The true translator however participates in the author's creative motion and then re-creates structure and sign systems by adapting the target language to the source as closely as intelligibility allows.

This potentially untranslatable terrain Celan very definitely shares with Rilke, his great predecessor and mentor in the radicalizing of poetic speech. Their personal biographies have practically nothing in common; however, the radical and exilic character of their linguistic conditions is very similar. It is no surprise then that the terrain is shared to a remarkable extent. There is, of course, one basic difference which more drastically affects their interpreters than their translators: Rilke's late poetry is often pervaded by a silence of fullness, Celan's by the muteness of non-existence.

German scholarship (particularly Ulrich Fülleborn) has repeatedly pointed to the affinities between Rilke and Celan but rarely focused on the differences. I should like to stress the desperate attempt at dialogue in both poets. Rilke (as narcissist) finds a way out, whereas Celan does not. We cannot truly gauge the enormous effort which Celan must have made to shatter, to use a euphemism, the solitude of the *lyrisches Ich* in his poetry. Thus, Celan's language is particled enough to be translatable bit by bit. Linguistic microorganisms do not, in themselves, constitute barriers to translation. To transpose intelligibly the matrix of an entire poem may however become an impossibility.

Once communication was severed, how could Celan continue to write? My answer is: After a certain point he did in fact not continue. Let Gottfried Benn spread his unsolicited and over-cited advice: "what you do not express does not exist," and let hundreds repeat it. We, as readers of Celan, must take note that there are existential experiences which neither at present nor in the future can be encoded in linguistic signs. *In that one sense*, Adorno's famous dictum about poetry after Auschwitz might have been right on target.

Briefly then, untranslatability is not a kind of interpretation, nor is it a lack or an impossibility of it. Untranslatability is not another word for hermeticism. Efforts at de-coding must *precede* any possible translation. I daresay if Celan had not written his late poetry during the onset of the interest in post-structuralist semiotics he would have received a great deal less "interpretation." Let's not forget that what for Mallarmé was, on an admittedly very high level, a prosodically interesting writing exercise (I refer to his poem "Rondel II" with the line "muet muet entre les ronds") became for Paul Celan, one of the translators of this text, a deadly accurate expression ("stumm-und-stumm"). That is the kind of noise ("das Dröhnen") with which the truth enters the squalls of metaphors. By comparison, Rilke's "reiner Widerspruch," pace-setting and linguistically exciting as it turned out to be, was indeed "lust" and was, most memorably, practiced on a rose's existence.

Celan has shown us that writing, tantamount to falling silent ("verstummen"), can be an active revocation and cancellation of existence. The days when mis-understandings, those stock items of comedy, were nothing but mis-takes, are over. At the turn of the century, Hofmannsthal's Lord Chandos had questioned the trustworthiness of language, and to Count Hans Karl Bühl the famous "Schwierige", eloquence seemed indecent by the end of World War I. His one important human relationship almost failed because of a series of misunderstandings. Paul Celan, by all reports, not only took every person at his word, but took them by every possible and barely possible meaning of that word. After Auschwitz, misunderstanding based upon severed or murdered communication has ceased to be comic, or even tragic; it simply has become deadly. Not only was language, i.e., German, a deadly language to Celan, but his very efforts to remove it from its particularly historical, i.e., Nazi encodation resulted in raising enormously high barriers to understanding for his readers. Muteness is a lethal form of silence. One can indeed translate a text's silence from one language into another. However, a poem that is built upon a matrix of muteness, a poem in which voices have been gradually, successively, or suddenly strangulated remains, I believe, untranslatable. "Verschweigen" (to cover with silence) is a transitive verb. One may choose to be silent about somthing that one *could* say in some language or other. "Verstummen", however, is intransitive.

Certainly, one *can* converse without words: with eyes, gestures, and hints. That, after all, is a form of communication. But once a person is ashes, all demonstrable communication with him or her (except through an act of remembrance) has come to an end. The dead do not have a language to be silent in. And remembrance in itself is untranslatable.

Chapter Two

Production and Reception

Translator and Author

Some Relationships

Leila Vennewitz
Vancouver, Canada

Some months ago, at a gathering of people interested in language and translation, a young man, a stranger to me, approached me and said rather sternly: "Are you the woman who translates Böll?" I acknowledged that I was, not knowing quite whether he expected me to apologize or to boast, so I waited. After some hesitation he went on: "Personally, *I* find translation extremely difficult. Whenever I try it, it never seems to come out right." I agreed that it was quite hard and said that of course I had been doing it for a great many years, and practice certainly made, if not perfect, at least better. He gave me a long, doubtful look and finally said: "Well, I suppose you know what you're doing," and with that he walked away. I later found out that he was a press photographer, and I wished I had known that at the time. I could have said to him: "Look, I haven't the slightest idea of how to take newspaper photographs. Why would you expect to be able to translate?" But that, of course, was our old friend *Treppenwitz*, and the opportune moment had passed.

However, at the time I was looking ahead to this event, and the little incident made me think that perhaps I could do worse than try, apart from assuring you that I do believe I know what I'm doing – to tell you why I believe that what I do is bound up with the relationships I have, or have had, with the authors whom I have translated. These relationships range from personal friendship to close association by correspondence, and in one case, where the author is no longer alive, simply with and through his work.

It was suggested that I talk to you about my work with a number of contemporary German authors, and I find that, whether I am to speak about one author or many, I can't do so comfortably without first saying something in general terms about how the function of translating works in me, and for me. So I propose first to outline what I think translation is, or ought to be, then to try and give you some idea of how I attempt to reach those goals, and lastly to say a little about a few German authors and how the content and style of their work relates to mine, as well as how my work relates to them and theirs.

Let me begin by giving you a definition of translation that I find very satisfactory, only I have to say that I have paraphrased the words of someone else, which only goes to show that I cannot refrain from translating even when I don't move outside my own language. G.M. Young has said, as quoted in *The Complete Plain Words*: "The final cause of speech is to get an idea as exactly as possible out of one mind into another."[1] For my present purposes I shall replace the word "speech" by "translation" and thus arrive at: The final cause of translation is to get an idea as exactly as possible out of one mind into another. I like this definition because it makes it clear that translation is not concerned only with such transitions as mouth to ear, speech to hearing, written or printed word to visual perception. Without one or more of these channels of communication, of course, no translation is possible, but they are not enough. What we are really concerned with is mind to mind, the getting of an idea as exactly as possible out of one mind into another. Now Young was not speaking of moving from one language to another, yet he might just as well have been, for when it comes to communicating we use the best available tools whether we are working in one language or two.

Many processes in translation are no different from those that go on in the daily speech of a monolingual person. George Steiner says in *After Babel*: "Inside or between languages, human communication equals translation."[2] Even when communication occurs between two people of similar age and background, every sentence uttered has to be filtered through layers upon layers of received ideas, of prejudice, preference, and conditioning. Normally this filtering process goes on automatically; we do it all the time without a thought. The sense of what is being said is our first concern, but we bring our sensibility to bear on the interpretation of that sense.

When we come to moving an idea out of one language into another, we find that, long before we begin actually to choose the words we need to use, we are involved in a continuous filtering process. First we filter what the author is saying through what we know of his preferences, his conditioning, even his received ideas and, possibly, prejudices. Obviously all these things will differ according to whether the author is a young man who has grown up in East Germany, say, and has chosen to leave East Germany and settle and write in West Germany; or whether the author is a middle-aged man living in the Rhineland where he was born and brought up, where he and all his writing belong. If the text is the work of a devout Catholic or a professed agnostic, the difference is going to make itself felt even if neither the Catholic nor the agnostic so much as mentions religion. Some readers of the original will perceive these differences; some will simply miss them. But for the translator to miss them can be disastrous. Let me quote again from George Steiner's *After Babel*: "To read fully is to restore all that one can of the immediacies of value and intent in which speech actually occurs."[3] If we substitute the word "translate" for "read," and the word "text" for "speech," we have the following paraphrase: To translate fully is to restore all that one can of the immediacies of value and intent in which the text actually occurs.

Assuming now that the translator is attuned to the author, how is he going to move those ideas out of the source language, across the void of no-language, into the receptor language so that nothing is lost? This journey is one of the most mysterious that the human mind is capable of making. To go back to my paraphrasing of Steiner's words: the phrase "to translate fully." This implies a profound exploration of the text, and I mean "profound" in an almost physical sense of depth, of descent. The image of descent has been used by many different writers. D.S. Carne-Ross, in his essay in *The Craft & Context of Translation*, writes: "[Translation] begins . . . at the pre-verbal level; the sentence, often the word, has to be dissolved, atomised, and its elements then reconstituted in a new form."[4] Montaigne spoke of "the spiral staircase of the self," and perhaps it is this spiral staircase that the translator descends in his search for the pre-verbal level. Virginia Woolf speaks of going "step by step down into the well" as she works on a new novel.

In speaking of the immediacies of value and intent, we can take the word "immediacies" to mean the "surroundings," the matrix of the text; "value" can be taken to mean the amount of emphasis to be conveyed, the nuances of weight the author wishes his words to carry, just as we speak of the "values" of the notes in a sonata. The word "intent" may be taken to mean the author's purpose in writing the text in the first place.

I spoke just now of the "void of no-language" through which the author's words must pass after leaving the source language and before reaching the receptor language. Denver Lindley, in *The Craft & Context of Translation*, analyzes what may happen here: "A moment comes in the translation of any important passage . . . when the author's intent hangs naked in the translator's mind. It has shed its original clothes and has not yet found new ones."[5]

What is going on while the author's intent is hanging naked in the translator's mind? Obviously it can't hang there indefinitely or we would have no translation. Yet it is here that part of the translation process takes place, in this area of no-language, so it may be worthwhile trying to account for the undeniable fact that out of this area comes a new creation, the source of which has very little to do with looking up words in a dictionary.

Let us therefore imagine a separate dimension, a kind of proto-source of intent on which both author and translator can draw. The author has been thinking of *something*, and the translator must think of the same thing: not merely of the text as it stands but of the intent behind the text. If it is true, as Charles Morgan has written, that two people come closest together not when they are thinking of each other but when they are thinking of the same thing, it follows that this "meeting of minds," if you like, has a good chance of producing an accurate reflection of the original and that the author will be well served by his translator.

Now I turn to the differences among authors that call for different skills on the part of the translator. First, there are no short cuts for the translator. Whether it be Uwe Johnson conjuring up life in New York in the sixties for a young German woman and her small daughter; or Walter Kempowski recreating life on the Rostock waterfront as it was at the turn of this century; or Heinrich Böll assembling a group portrait in the prewar and war years in Cologne; or Martin Walser moving about inside the head of a real estate agent on the shores of Lake Constance as easily as if about his own study: all these intents, once translation is embarked upon, have no choice but to travel that mysterious route along which, at some point, they will hang naked, in the area of no-language, in the translator's mind. Whether we stress that translation is a craft rather than an art, or an art as well as a craft, the intuition required for one aspect of translation, and the skills required for another, all form part of the relationship between author and translator.

The German authors I am about to discuss are: Walter Kempowski, Martin Walser, Heinrich Böll, Jurek Becker, Franz Fühmann, and Uwe Johnson.

Franz Fühmann's book, titled in English *Twenty-Two Days or Half a Lifetime*, is an account of the three weeks he spent in 1972 in Budapest, a summing-up of the place in life at which he feels he has arrived in middle age. After what he calls a fascist upbringing, he spent years – after capture by the Russians during World War

II – at a Soviet anti-fascist school, and the implicit dialectic in the switch he was caused to make in his philosophy runs through the whole book. His often somewhat fanciful style, unorthodox punctuation, fragments of concrete poetry, his excursions into real and legendary aspects of Hungarian history, his surrealist descriptions of dreams, his almost visionary waking experiences that may be all metaphor but might be all fact: all these invite the reader to read on many levels. He quotes Wittgenstein as follows: "The limits of my language represent the limits of my world," and Fühmann, in pushing out the limits of language as far as he can, is also pushing out the limits of his world to embrace far more than socialist or communist ideology. Let me read you a short passage from a description of his arrival in Budapest by train from Berlin:

> In the mirror of the cabinet over the washbasin the scenery proceeds in reverse to the movement offered the eye through the window, and if outside it seems to be running away from you, in the mirror it is coming toward you. The future manifests itself as the present; form and duration of the world outside are doubled: a magical gain, but this duplication also causes vertigo, one is no longer sure of one's place; the question of forward or backward becomes meaningless and, at the line where mirror and window meet the divided world runs together, flowing into itself and canceling itself out: antimatter and matter soundlessly meeting in a shimmer, each soundlessly destroying itself in the other.

And the following is an illustration of metaphor embedded in a flight of fancy:

> And in my room the wardrobe: a chamber designed by Frankenstein. . ., an oaken dungeon, an Anak's coffin, a Goliath's cubbyhole: ten feet high, six feet wide, three feet deep, no shelves, and clear across the cavernous interior a rod as thick as your arm, and a bolt suitable for Bluebeard's seventh door. But this bolt is on the inside, not on the outside, and anyone guessing the Open Sesame of its secret would experience the thousand-and second night.

Fühmann's ability to swing from one level to another, like Tarzan from branch to branch with only his own momentum to sustain him, requires a flexibility in translation that will reflect this diversity.

The last excerpt from Franz Fühmann that I would like to read tells us about the eternal quandary of the imaginative writer:

> Sudden memory of having dreamed last night . . . of buying an orchid . . ., and then, as if an invisible curtain were jerked aside, the memory that, earlier in the dream, I had walked through a forest, a forest with a clear green sheet of water under which lay the interlacing red paths. . . . Silence; the knee-deep water lay motionless, and I was afraid to enter it; I stood in a trance at its edge, looking in rapture at the indescribably deep-green purity and, below it, the ornament of the paths as they ran together and apart; not a sound was to be heard, not a tremor, not a movement; I stood and looked and reached mechanically for the notebook in my pocket, to register this scene, but put it back again immediately, thinking: No, don't write! Don't turn this magic into paper. It was the determination . . . to have a piece of life that does not dissolve into ink, with no ulterior motive of literary usefulness.[6]

The translator's relationship with Franz Fühmann, then, must be one of appreciation of his quandary. "My generation," Fühmann writes, "has arrived at Socialism via Auschwitz. All reflection on our change must begin at the gas chamber, and nowhere else."

Uwe Johnson was born in Pomerania in 1934; in 1959 he moved to the West, first for some years to West Berlin and later to England. At the time I started translating *Jahrestage*, in English *Anniversaries*, not all the volumes, of which there were to be four, had been completed by the author. This meant that I found myself in midstream with the author, he well ahead of me but with an eye to the translation that was on its way. He became, I believe, almost as involved in my translation as in his original and minutely scrutinized the translation before publication, which in my experience is a fairly rare occurrence and can only be undertaken, of course, when the author has more than ordinary knowledge of the receptor language. This is the only time I have worked quite in this way, and I found it posed some difficulties. One problem was that, on asking for clarification, I was often told: "Ah, you'll be coming to that later, it'll all clear up," and more than once I had to ask Uwe Johnson to clear up the mystery then and there, it being one thing to keep the reader on tenterhooks but quite another to do the same with the translator.

Nevertheless, there were many very good things about translating Uwe Johnson. Having lived for two years in New York, he speaks very good English and feels completely at home writing about New York. Much of *Anniversaries* takes place, too, in Mecklenburg, where he also lived, and in England, parts of which he knows well. This familiarity gave a ring of authenticity to his writing that was not hard to convey in English just because it *was* authentic, and certainty on the part of the author unquestionably makes itself felt as soon as the translator starts to work on the text.

I would like to read you a paragraph from *Anniversaries* that will give you the flavor of Uwe Johnson in translation: his description of a sweltering day in New York. It is an example of what I call his "cumulative rhythmic style," a favorite device of his:

September 9, 1967. Saturday
Justice almost prevails in New York this morning. The air is motionless. The air cannot move under stationary heat masses in the upper atmosphere, since yesterday it has been unable to rise into the cold and shed the dirt pumped into it by the city from power plants, gasworks, chimney stacks, car motors, jet engines, and ships: the inversion has clamped an impenetrable dome over the city. The accumulated dirt from soot, fly ash, hydrocarbons, carbon monoxide, sulfur dioxide, nitrous oxide, is no respecter of persons and seeps through cracks of windows into eyes, into skin folds, dries out throats, shrivels mucous membranes, exerts pressure on the heart, blackens tea and seasons food, creates additional work for lung specialists, shoe shiners, car washers, window cleaners, and for Mr. Fang Liu, in his basement shop off Broadway, who accepts the Cresspahl laundry from Marie with deft, eager gestures. A few people can hide behind sealed double glazing and high-powered air conditioners: imprisoned in their bare, fusty towers on the East Side, they miss the lurid clouds painted by the humidity beyond Riverside Park, miss the dun rags of haze draping the Hudson. In every store on Broadway where Marie walks around with her shopping cart, the mere word "pollution" will invariably yield her some con-

versation as well as the New Yorker's pride in the unparalleled difficulty of life in New York, mutual sympathy, sighs can be exchanged and smiles bartered when she pushes her hair back from her perspiring brow with her forearm. Outside, on the hot, darkened street, she will feel as if her face were plunging into a wall of steaming water.[7]

Jurek Becker spent most of his early years in the Lodz ghetto and in concentration camps. When he submitted his novel *Schlaflose Tage* to his publisher in East Germany he was asked by the censors to make substantial changes. Unable to acquiesce without destroying the very core of his argument, he moved to the West and published his book in the Federal Republic of Germany.

Unlike Franz Fühmann's book, *Sleepless Days* (the English title of *Schlaflose Tage*) is all of a piece, a translator's delight. An indictment of hypocrisy within the school system of the German Democratic Republic, it begins lightly enough and ends tragically though triumphantly, yet the development throughout is one of seamless exposition. The translator must become the intimate friend of Simrock, a schoolteacher. Once you have identified with Simrock's fear, on the very first page, that the slight but terribly sudden pain he feels is the signal for a heart attack – "Simrock felt like someone plunging from glowing health into illness" – once you have shared this with Simrock you have no difficulty accompanying him all the rest of the way, since that pain is what jolts him out of his sleepwalking docility and makes him start questioning and rejecting all the values by which he has been living.

Becker's great skill is in knowing exactly where to apply the feather touch and where to bear down with the weight of anguish. The entire story of loss, and love, and loss again flows from that moment in the classroom when, "for the first time in his life, Simrock became aware of his heart." The logical consistency of the unfolding tale asks for a similar consistency in translation, and it is not hard to reflect the rounding-off of the story in the last few lines so that they reverberate in the mind of the reader in English just as they do in the mind of the reader in German. The last lines of the book are:

> He immediately remembered his little pain in the classroom and his
> great fear that Death was breathing down his neck. He thought that,
> if he tried to see the whole affair in a favorable light, the anxiety
> born at that time and on which he was still feeding might after all
> have been a gain.[8]

I come now to the three other German writers I mentioned:
Walter Kempowski, Martin Walser, and Heinrich Böll.

Walter Kempowski, born 1929, lives in the country between
Hamburg and Bremen. His book *Aus großer Zeit*, published in
English as *Days of Greatness*,[9] is saturated with the sights and scents
and sounds of Germany's northern coastline – that is, of a coastline
running along what are now East and West Germany.

Kempowski is the writer par excellence of nostalgia. With him,
it is a question not merely of a writer in search of the past but of a
writer who succeeds in finding the past. In *Days of Greatness*, voice
after voice – and he uses many voices – evokes not only modes of
speech, family mores, political and public events of the turn of the
century in Rostock and Hamburg, but also a sense of the more
remote past that preceded the immediate past of seventy to eighty
years ago. In addition, he is a writer of the five senses, conveying
with extraordinary immediacy such things as the *feel* of fabrics, the
sweep of a woman's hair, the *pungency* of a basket of fish, the *taste*
of fruit fresh from the garden, the *sound* of carriage wheels on
cobblestones, and of course the translator has to be sure the reader
will be able to touch, see, smell, taste, and hear just as well in
English as in German.

It is up to the translator of such a work as *Days of Greatness* to
find a counterpart for each voice, whether it be the narrator, or his
grandfather, his father, his oh so English aunt, or a schoolmate, a
family friend, the family dressmaker, the housekeeper, a wartime
comrade: all of these and more make contributions to the steadily
advancing story, which is both novel and family document. The
mother, for instance, when she was still what used to be called a

"young matron," appears in a variety of lights depending on the person who is talking about her. The narrator sees her as one would expect: a figure ensconced in her "place" – that is, her place in life, in her son's young life and, physically, inside her house, like this:

> In the white villa . . . with stuccoed ceilings but no fireplace – full of heavy brocade drapes with tasseled cords, with the unframed portrait of Bismarck, that greatest diplomat of all time, on a carved easel, with holly and quantities of bric-a-brac, albums, little boxes, round or oblong, lying around as if just used or about to be used - in this drape-shrouded domesticity stands his mother, looking into the ornate mirror and patting her waist smooth. She has a cold face and wears her black hair pinned high: it's time the dressmaker came again, one really hasn't a thing to wear."[10]

The description is as chilly as the chill in her face. But then we very soon have another picture of her, and this time it is by a young woman applying breathlessly for the position of housekeeper to this mistress of a great household:

> I dressed quickly, a simple navy-blue suit and a white hat, and off I hurried. My heart was really beating fast, for the Kempowskis were prominent people and lived in a high-class neighborhood.
>
> So I went there and rang the bell, and I'm standing there in the front hall when she comes sailing down the staircase, Madam herself. "Is it starting all over again this morning?" she said, for seventy-five girls had answered the advertisement, and they had been besieging the house for days. "Is it really starting all over again this morning?" she said, and: "Would you mind going into the drawing room, my husband has to have his breakfast first."
>
> So down I sat in the Biedermeier drawing room – I've gone Biedermeier myself now – and looked at their stuff: the chandelier and the lovely furniture, all polished. The alcove had a heavy green velvet curtain across it, and there were photos everywhere, on the sewing table and on the chest of drawers, photos of relatives and friends and of Madam herself, taken at a spa, in the park, leaning against a birch tree wearing a straw hat. . .
>
> So I sat there and waited, and when her husband had finished his breakfast she saw him off, the cab was already waiting at the door.

And then she swept in again and said: "Well, now it's *your* turn..."[11] Later we have a singer, a tenor from Hamburg who was her lover, but not explicitly so, and again a twitch is given to the figure of this difficult but passionate and always memorable woman so that we see her from a slightly different angle. And at other times we hear her own inner voice, her own self-justifications and bitternesses.

Throughout the book Kempowski scatters nursery rhymes, jingles, couplets from old songs, like peppercorns across the pages, and I had to ransack the attic of my childhood memories in much the same way, I suppose, that the author did his. I must say I enjoyed coming up with counterparts that usually took the place of the German originals neatly enough. A few were translations, but the majority were what I hope were good matches: look-alikes, or sound-alikes, for obviously the translator has to pluck the chords of his reader's memory in the reader's language if he is to set off the same response as the author does in communicating with his reader in his language.

And here I would like to say, as a kind of aside, that among the compensations that are alleged to accrue as one gets older is the undeniable one that accrues to the translator with the passage of time: the simple advantage of the straight accumulation of experience and memories. *Days of Greatness* depends more than any book I have ever translated, I think, on the translator not being removed by too many decades from the era the book so masterfully evokes. This is not to say that the translator *must* have immediate experience of the material he is working on, any more than that would be true of the author of the original; but the translator is concerned with removing barriers to communication, and if he does not himself have to cope with the barrier of unfamiliarity his translation is more likely to ring true.

Martin Walser, born 1927, who lives on the north shore of Lake Constance, writes from the inside out. In *Ein fliehendes Pferd* (in English, *Runaway Horse*[12]), as well as *Das Schwanenhaus* (published in English as *The Swan Villa*[13]), his story is unfolded almost entirely by means of interior monologue. In a third book, written between these two, called *Seelenarbeit*,[14], he makes less use of interior monologue, but even in descriptive passages he conveys the subjectivity that permeates his work. Here is a brief passage:

> The night was clear. Xaver swung the car voluptuously up the curving road that led to his own part of the country. . . . He switched off the headlights. The moonlight, the blossoming trees, and his almost white car made a more harmonious whole without light. He could see just as well at night as during the day. And at this hour there wasn't a soul on the road. Yes there was – Friday! The customers from the inn. Reluctantly he switched his lights on again. Now he could see only what the light sawed out of the darkness. Turning off the motor he glided down into the village with just enough impetus to bring him up the rise to the farmhouse. His dog Tell was standing there as if he had been waiting day and night for a week. Xaver thrust his hand into the dog's fur and caressed him. Tell tried to tunnel his way into some part of Xaver. The dog snuffled and whimpered as quietly as he could, but Xaver had to ask him to be even quieter. Tell groaned. Xaver hugged him. Tell trembled. Xaver dug his fingers into the fur. Suddenly Tell knocked Xaver over. Dorle the cat ran up and rubbed herself against his leg with arched back. As Xaver approached the kitchen door, it opened. Agnes said in a whisper: "How late you are."[15]

In translating this passage the translator must feel almost physically the tension that leads up to the wife's whispered remark: "How late you are." Is it a rebuke? Or is it merely a statement? And the statement, or the rebuke, must be led up to exactly as in the German, the tension stretching seamlessly all the way from the clarity of the night to the domesticity of the dog's fur and the cat's back, as if the eye of a camera were sweeping the night sky and the landscape, and coming to rest in a farm yard.

And now finally Heinrich Böll. Of those authors whom I translate, he is probably the one who conveys what most readers think of as "flavor," "atmosphere." I am not saying that I personally believe this to be so, but I find that is how most people perceive him. How, Germans have asked me, does one convey that flavor, that feel of the place, of the time? How does that special atmosphere of the Rhineland, its people, their particular brand of humor, the way they speak and look and eat and go about their daily lives, the atmosphere of wartime Germany and postwar and present-day Germany, "come through" in English? They feel this must be an impossible task for a translator, just as some might doubt whether any translation into German could ever convey the atmosphere of a particular region of Canada.

But this, strange to say, does not seem to be one of the translator's major problems. The more pronounced the flavor of the original, the more readily is that flavor conveyed into another language. This is not done by means of dialect or jargon words; it is something that occurs naturally when the translator shares the author's original experience. Heinrich Böll is, among so many other things, a very funny writer. His humor is not hard to translate. If you find it funny in German, you laugh as you translate it, and it turns out to be funny in English too. It does not even "suffer a sea change": it simply becomes what Böll would have written had English been his native tongue.

One thing Heinrich Böll never is, is tentative. It is the tentative writer, the writer who is groping, who is striving to overcome his own ambivalences, who causes a problem for the translator. I don't hesitate to say that the passages in a work that pose the most difficulty for the translator are those that must have posed problems for the author.

Heinrich Böll is a totally "prepared" writer. Starting with the accumulation of scraps of paper bearing his notes which, he tells us in *Irish Journal*, he keeps stored in a sewing basket, all the way to the systematic manner in which he finally transforms those scraps of paper into literature, he knows what he is doing and where his work is going. The "gestation period," if you like, of Böll's works is usually long; the pile in the sewing basket accumulates, and when he is ready the material is all there – and it is *then* that the "sea change" takes place.

Why then – assuming the translator masters the tools of his craft

– should it be impossible to convey Böll's styles as well as content into another language? I am not saying it is easy: in fact, I am reminded of the carpenter who was asked by the poet and translator William Jay Smith as he watched him at work whether what the carpenter was doing wasn't difficult. The carpenter replied: "It's not difficult, it's just hard." I recently read a new German translation of Jane Austen's *Emma*, by Ursula and Christian Grawe, and it is a triumph. It might be thought impossible to produce a convincing German version of something as quintessentially English as the style and content of a book by Jane Austen, but convincing is exactly what that translation is.

Lastly, to show how Heinrich Böll has moved through, and even among, a number of styles since he first began writing at the end of World War II, and how the translator must be able to move with him, I would like to read you two passages: the first from a relatively early work, *Irish Journal*, which, as *Irisches Tagebuch*, was published in 1957, and the second from a more recent novel, *Fürsorgliche Belagerung*, published in 1982 as *The Safety Net*.[17] He starts *Irish Journal* with a description of his arrival by boat in Ireland from Liverpool:

> As soon as I boarded the steamer I could see, hear, and smell that I had crossed a frontier. I had seen one of England's gentle, lovely sides: Kent, almost bucolic - I had barely skimmed the topographical marvel that is London - then seen one of England's gloomier sides, Liverpool - but here on the steamer there was no more England: here there was already a smell of peat, the sound of throaty Celtic from between decks and the bar, here Europe's social order was already assuming new forms: poverty was no longer "no disgrace," it was neither honor nor disgrace: it was - as an element of social awareness - as irrelevant as wealth; trouser creases had lost their sharp edge, and the safety pin, that ancient Celtic clasp, had come into its own again. Where the button had looked like a full stop, put there by the tailor, the safety pin had been hung on like a comma; a sign of improvisation, it draped the material in folds, where the button had prevented this. I also saw it used to attach price tags, lengthen suspenders, replace cufflinks, finally used as a weapon by a small boy to pierce a man's trouser seat: the boy was

surprised, frightened because the man did not react in any way; the boy carefully tapped the man with his forefinger to see if he was still alive: he was still alive, and patted the boy laughingly on the shoulder.[18]

There we have an observation of an external scene. Nearly a quarter of a century later, in 1979, came *Fürsorgliche Belagerung*. Shortly after the beginning of this novel there is also an observation, but an observation of an internal scene, the thoughts of an old man who has just that day, against his real desires, been elected president of the Publishers' Association in the Federal Republic of Germany, a position that will inevitably expose him to terrorist threats and possibly even murderous attacks:

> What he was saying, ad-libbing, came out almost automatically, prefabricated, allowing him to think of other things, to determine at what point his fear had suddenly left him: most likely at the moment when he realized the inevitability of being elected. This would hoist him into a position where his fear should have been intensified, and - so his thoughts ran while he gave yet another interview - instinct had told him that the better course was to have no fear at all rather than more. No fear at all, merely curiosity; the fear that had weighed on him for months, the fear for his life, for Käthe's life, for Sabine's and Kit's lives, was gone. Of course they would get him, probably even kill him, and there remained only the suspense of wondering: who, and how? And what he felt for Sabine had been transformed from fear into concern. He had reason to be concerned about the children.[19]

A period of twenty-two years lies between the writing of these two passages, yet they are connected as if by a span of which each segment is linked to the preceding one and the following one. Both passages are analytical: in one, *Irish Journal*, the eye is turned outward; in the other, *The Safety Net*, it is turned inward. And in each case the eye of the translator must move in the same direction as the author's. –

I hope I have given you the impression, or possibly even convinced some of you, that translation is not, as I understand it was once called by a former President of American PEN, "the impossible art," but that on the contrary, if translator and author will, in

E.M. Forster's words, "only connect," translation may serve the author well and deserve to be called "the possible art."

NOTES

1. Sir Ernest Gowers, *The Complete Plain Words*. Rev. ed. by Sir Bruce Fraser. (London: H.M. Stationery Office, 1973) p. 1.

2. George Steiner, *After Babel* (New York & London: Oxford UP, 1975) p. 47.

3. *Ibid.*, p. 24.

4. William Arrowsmith & Roger Shattuck, eds., *The Craft & Context of Translation* (Austin: U of Texas Press, 1961) p. 4.

5. *Ibid.*, p. 161.

6. Franz Fühmann, *Twenty-two Days or Half a Lifetime*. Trans. Leila Vennewitz (Berlin: Seven Seas, 1980) pp. 14, 17, 173, 197. From the German *Zweiundzwanzig Tage oder Die Hälfte des Lebens* (Rostock: Hinstorff, 1973).

7. Uwe Johnson, *Anniversaries*. Trans. Leila Vennewitz (New York & London: Harcourt, 1974f.) p. 48. From: *Jahrestage*, part I (Frankfurt: Suhrkamp, 1970f).

8. Jurek Becker, *Sleepless Days*. Trans. Leila Vennewitz (New York & London: Harcourt, 1979). From: *Schlaflose Tage* (Frankfurt: Suhrkamp, 1978).

9. Walter Kempowski, *Days of Greatness*. Trans. Leila Vennewitz (New York: Knopf, 1981; London: Secker & Warburg, 1982). From: *Aus großer Zeit* (Hamburg: Knaus, 1978).

10. *Ibid.*, p. 35.

11. *Ibid.*, p. 40.

12. Martin Walser, *Runaway Horse*. Trans. Leila Vennewitz. (New York: Holt, Rinehart & Winston, 1980; London: Secker & Warburg, 1980). From: *Ein fliehendes Pferd* (Suhrkamp, 1978).

13. Martin Walser, *The Swan Villa*. Trans. Leila Vennewitz (New York: Holt, Rinehart & Winston, 1982). From: *Das Schwanenhaus* (Suhrkamp, 1980).

14. Martin Walser, *Seelenarbeit* (Suhrkamp, 1979).

15. *Ibid.*, p. 87.

16. Heinrich Böll, *Irish Journal*. Trans. Leila Vennewitz (New York: McGraw-Hill, 1967). From: *Irisches Tagebuch* (Cologne: Kiepenheuer & Witsch, 1957).

17. Heinrich Böll, *The Safety Net*. Trans. Leila Vennewitz (New York: Knopf, 1982; London: Secker & Warburg, 1982.)

18. *Irish Journal*, p. 1.

19. *The Safety Net*, p. 3.

Literary Translation
and the Academic Curriculum

Gerhart Teuscher,
McMaster University

What place could there be for literary translation in the academic curriculum? Should it perhaps be taught as a regular course in every department of language and literature and at every university? And if so, as an undergraduate course, or at the graduate level? Should new university programmes be established to train literary translators, and if so, what should these programmes look like? Or will it perhaps be submitted that literary translators cannot really be "trained," that literary translation is not a "teachable" subject at all and that courses on literary translation can therefore not form part of any academic curriculum?

For practical purposes, I propose to limit myself to outlining our own programme involving literary translation here at McMaster, and to making a few general comments on the topic. I would like to talk about the McMaster programme also because I have been involved in it from the beginning, i.e., since the late seventies.

For several years we had noticed a growing interest amongst our students in making translation a part of their study of language and literature and in particular in selecting for their thesis a topic involving the translation of German literary prose into English. We therefore decided to establish in our graduate programme an option in literary translation. A student interested in this option will, in consultation with his or her supervisor, choose an author — most likely a contemporary author — and undertake to translate a particular work, or parts of a work, or perhaps several short stories. The student meets regularly with the supervisor to discuss the completed portions of the translation and to make any necessary changes. Two additional readers are then asked to go over the revised translations and to add their comments and suggestions, which are in turn incorporated into the translation.

While the translation constitutes the central part of the thesis, the complete thesis consists of a good deal more than the translation. There is to be an introductory section containing a critical discussion of the text in relation to the author's other major works, and a short analysis of literary theme and style. (I should also mention that the student is expected to demonstrate a good knowledge of the author and the major secondary literature in the oral defence of the thesis.) The translation itself is to be followed by a detailed and critical commentary on specific difficulties encountered in the process of translating. Ideally, this commentary will be expanded into an enlightened discussion of major inherent elements and qualities of the text and strive to offer some new and valid insights gained in the process of close reading and competent translating, thereby making the translation an exciting and worthwhile linguistic and literary exercise.[1]

We also agreed in our Department that students choosing this translation option should be offered a formal introduction into the art and techniques of translating literary prose, in the form of a special course. This course, which was taught for the first time in 1980 and is offered every year, covers one term and consists of thirteen seminar meetings of two hours each. The main emphasis in the course is on the critical analysis and translation of selected texts of a literary nature, so as to provide the students with the necessary skills and techniques and to increase their awareness of the problems and limitations of translating. To be more specific: During the first two sessions there is a short survey of the history and theory of translation, together with an introduction into a number of important current reference works. In addition, excerpts of approximately one page in length of established English translations of German literary prose are examined together in class and compared with the originals. Where several translations are available, these are themselves compared to each other and to the original work. A close study is undertaken of original and translations, to see where the various problems are and how these have been solved, and to gauge the range and the limits of translatability.

Following this initial comparative approach, German texts only are distributed, to be rendered into English individually for the next class. The various versions produced are then critically discussed together, and the relative merits and possible shortcomings of each version are carefully weighed.[2] In addition to taking an active part in these discussions, students are normally expected to contribute to the class, by completing three individual assignments: (1) They are given an article of moderate length dealing with an important aspect of literary translation and are asked to present a summary and critique in class.[3] (2) They select, in consultation with the instructor, a literary text of approximately one printed page in length, for translation into English. This translation is then discussed individually with the instructor and, if necessary, revised, and is presented in class after the other students have had an opportunity to examine both original and translation. (3) In lieu of a term paper each student selects a literary text of between ten and fifteen pages for translation into English. The third assignment is each student's main contribution to the course and forms the basis for the term mark. The students are allowed ample time for this main assignment, which may be handed in as late as several weeks after the end of the term. Needless to say, all students are expected to try their very best here, in order to demonstrate their thorough understanding of the German and their competence in producing a faithful, well-written English version. The translation is to include a footnoted analysis and a short, critical discussion of the main problems encountered.[4]

Discussing the individually prepared translation assignments in class usually turns out to be the most productive and rewarding part of the course. The students go over their translations, sentence by sentence, phrase by phrase, word by word, explaining why they chose this formulation over that and defending their choice against the critical comments of the others, who have both original and translation before them. Invariably we run out of time and finally quit, feeling exhausted and at the same time exhilarated and thrilled, at having individually and collectively grappled with the problems of the text, and at having found at times a phrase or a wording that seemed just right in the English — and coming away much of the time with a better understanding and greater appreciation of a literary work of art.[5]

I would like to conclude my comments with a few suggestions about the possible future of literary translation in the curriculum: First of all, we should accept the fact that there is no urgent need to establish in all or even in the majority of our language department, special programmes designed to train professional literary translators. Having said this, I would strongly recommend that all advanced language courses include a literary translation component — not to train translators, but to help improve the students' grammar, syntax and style, heighten their awareness of linguistic difficulties, and increase their understanding and appreciation of literature. Regular literary translation courses might be offered in graduate programmes, primarily again with a view to strengthening language competence at an advanced level, but also as an incentive and as practical training for those students who might want to write a thesis involving the translation of a literary work of art, perhaps in preparation for a later career in the field. Also at the graduate level, more emphasis might presumably be placed on translation-oriented research, on such topics as the reception of translated literature in other countries, and in particular on how such reception is influenced by the quality of the translations available. This could probably be done very well in cooperation with departments or inter-departmental committees offering comparative literature studies.

A valid model for such studies might be the research programme carried out at the *Institut für romanische Philologie*, Salzburg University, under the direction of Professor Mario Wandruszka, on the topic of "Verfälschung von Literatur durch Übersetzung in andere Sprachen" (i.e. the distortion of literature through translation into other languages.) Professor Wandruszka and his team have focussed on the kind of reception accorded to Austrian writers such as Hofmannsthal, Kafka, Musil, Zweig, Cannetti, Schnitzler, Bachmann, and Handke as translated authors, and they have asked: Is the image conveyed internationally through the translations in fact a true reflection of the original work? Is this image not perhaps changed or even distorted in the process of translation? And, if so, what are the changes? What is lost in the process?

My last suggestion may sound rather utopian; it is, nevertheless, submitted with a good deal of hopeful enthusiasm: Is it conceivable that within Canada and the United States, an international centre might be established at one of our universities, ideally with the support and encouragement of the government and of professional translation associations and modelled on what has been established in Europe, at the German town of Straelen near the Dutch border? I am referring of course to the *Europäisches Übersetzer-Kollegium*, which has been set up as a unique translation centre offering working space for a number of practising translators, editors, and translation researchers representing different languages, so they can stay and work at the centre for certain periods of time and leave to the centre the result of their work, such as notes, manuscripts, and working copies. Translation, related research, publication and gathering of documentation are carried out at the centre, which has its own 25,000 volume library and a computerized documentation facility and whose declared purpose is , "auf den Gebieten der Übersetzung literarischer und wissenschaftlicher Werke den internationalen Kulturaustausch zu fördern und den Gedanken der Völkerverständigung zu stärken."[6]

Of course, no university programme in literary translation, no matter how thorough or how varied, will ever turn out or need to turn out large numbers of competent professionals who will in due course corner the market for literary works. However, while much of the best in this challenging field will continue to be produced by relatively few and uniquely gifted people who are often authors themselves, we may well see in the years ahead some of our own graduates who will go on to fame in their profession as literary translators.

NOTES

1. There is also a less comprehensive option available to our students, consisting of a translation *project* of no fewer than thirty pages. Such a project consists of a translated text with commentary, the main emphasis to be placed on accuracy and style of the translation. This option has been popular with students interested in trying out their translation skills, without investing the considerable time required to complete a regular translation thesis.

2. The first text we looked at together in one year was an excerpt from Heinrich Böll's *Gruppenbild mit Dame*, together with the translation by Leila Vennewitz, his Canadian translator. This was followed by several passages from Mark Twain's *Huckleberry Finn*, together with three recent German translations; in other words, we were doing a study in reverse, as it were, in order to point to the problems the foreign translators faced and to see how they had each solved them — or failed to solve them. Then came the first general translation assignment without a parallel English version, from a story by Jurek Becker, *New Yorker Woche*.

3. This presentation also serves to offer temporary "relief" from the intensive — and exhausting — translation work. To give two examples: (a) Leslies Coup [Interview with Professor Leslie Willson, University of Texas at Austin, about the American Literary Translators Association], *Börsenblatt* Nr. 13, Feb. 13, 1979, pp. 293-95. (b) Herr seiner Zeit und Knecht seiner Einkünfte. Das Handwerk des Übersetzers. Aus einer Rede in eigener Sache, by Curt Meyer-Clason, *Frankfurter Allgemeine Zeitung*, No. 215, Sept. 15, 1979.

4. Here are a few examples of texts from which excerpts have been chosen by the students for the major translation assignments: (1) Theodor Fontane: *Der Stechlin*, chapter one. (2) Arthur Schnitzler: *Lieutenant Gustl* (3) Heinrich Mann: *Das Wunderbare*. (4) Fritz Rudolf Fries: *Der Läufer auf dem Dach*.

5. Class size and student preparation of course play a vital part part in making this result possible. I have found that six or seven students is about the right number, because this makes it possible to fit in several student presentations and still have ample time for general class discussions. As far as linguistic competence

is concerned, a student with four years of solid language and literature should be sufficiently prepared for the course. Ideally, one would look for a high degree of linguistic and literary competence, a superior ability to approach a text with sensitivity, controlled imagination, and critical curiosity. Needless to say, a solid general knowledge, a superior command of the target language and a good knowledge of its literature are equally desirable.

6. Quoted from a recent *Kollegium* brochure describing the centre's "Vereins-zweck".

A Basic Course in Translation

Barbara S. Wright
University of Connecticutt

I am expected to talk to you about the methodology of literary translation. But before I get to the main body of my talk, I would like to explain briefly what I am *not* talking about here. By "methodology of literary translation" I do not mean the translating of literature as a pedagogical device to help a student master a foreign language, or as a device to test a student's mastery of a foreign language. Nor am I talking about translating literature in the classroom for the purpose of educating students to understand or appreciate literature. Finally, I am not here today to present a full-scale theory of translation methodology, though some sort of theoretical approach may perhaps be inferred from my remarks.

What I *am* talking about here is translation as a particular kind of language skill which, like other language skills, can to a degree be cultivated and enhanced by the thoughtful and goal-directed use of specific kinds of exercises and assignments. I prefer to leave theoretical expositions to more abstract thinkers and talk to you today about my concrete experiences and practices as a teacher of translation.

And that in turn requires just a word about my students. When they come to my course, they have generally completed the equivalent of three years of college German. I assume they know enough German to avoid gross errors of understanding or transference in a passage of moderate difficulty. Unlike European students, mine do not contemplate a career in translation *per se*; if they did, they probably wouldn't be studying at Storrs in the first place. Instead, my students may wish to sample translation, to see whether it might interest them as a career. Or — more often — they aim to acquire a language skill of potential vocational value which they can then offer to a prospective employer as just one in a "package" of job skills. At the same time, though, these *are* liberal arts students, and a taste of literary translation along with business letters or technical articles is not out of place.

My students have time and interest only for the rudiments, and under such circumstances it makes little sense for me to take a highly theoretical approach. What my students want and need, in the course of one or at most two semesters, is a straightforward, practically-oriented introduction to principles and techniques of translation. I firmly believe that such a thorough introduction is possible only if they have the experience of translating all three of the "text types" which Katharina Reiss distinguishes: "expressive" or literary texts and "operative" (or perhaps "manipulative") texts, as well as "informational" or fact-oriented texts. But more of that in a moment.

Finally, I probably ought to say something about my personal prejudices regarding literature and literary translation. I prefer to think of literature as just one point on a language continuum. It *is* different from other uses of language, but it is not wholly and necessarily "other." And it is precisely the borderline genres — letters, diaries, essays and anecdotes, for example — that have always particularly fascinated me. Similarly I view literary translation as a special branch of the translating craft, one requiring special gifts and a special creativity, but not impossible to approach via more prosaic paths. This is also evident in my translation methodology, where literary texts are integrated into the curriculum and students must learn to use translation principles and techniques appropriately here as in other areas.

But *what* principles? *What* techniques? How do you go about convincing the student, in a realm as elusive as translation, that though there is not and never will be a single "best" translation, still there are criteria that can be applied and judgements that must be made to distinguish the clearly wrong translation from the unsatisfactory rendering, and to identify the optimal equivalent? That the instructor is not simply being arbitrary? It is precisely the interworking of objective and subjective elements in translation which makes the learning process at times so frustrating for the student, who wants a clear "yes" or "no" and a plausible explanation.

My point of departure, as I said a moment ago, is decidedly pragmatic. Several years ago, I decided to offer a course in translation from German to English. I would order a couple of textbooks and somehow everything would be all right. What embarrassing naiveté! There were no texbooks to be had for my purpose, and everything did not turn out all right. I shudder now to recall that first time through. I had a perfectly fatal touch when it came to selecting suitable passages for translation. Simply discussing our work pre- and post-mortem didn't satisfy any of us. And producing a single "model" translation at the end of each unit seemed a gross simplification of the problems and questions we had encountered at virtually every turn of phrase.

Finally, after a particularly frustrating session toward the end of that semester, I decided to bring in a sort of schematic, step-by-step explanation of how to recognize, decode and translate that peculiarly German phenomenon, the extended adjective construction, into sensible English. The explanation was accompanied by some fairly preposterous sample sentences which I had made up to drive the point home — and students loved it. They asked for more exercises pinpointing specific problems in the transfer from German to English, and before the semester was out, we had done anticipatory constructions and a variety of uses of "es," as well as some exercises in levels of style. At that point I still didn't have any easily digestible "principles" or "techniques" for my students, by now I had an inkling of the direction I should go in.

Since then I have made a sort of morbid hobby out of going to the book exhibits at professional conferences and asking all the publishing houses if they have a textbook on translation practice from German to English. They have invariably answered "no." If any of you know of such a book, perhaps a *samizdat* edition circulating secretly somewhere, I would be most grateful to hear about it. Professor Wilss's remarks suggest that we are still a long way from such a text. The next question I ask is "Would you like to publish mine?" The answer to that question, alas, is also invariably "no." If you could show us a market for such a book, they say, why then we would be happy to consider it. And I reply that if they published such a book there would be more translation courses and, obviously, more market. Clearly, only fools like myself rush in where angels fear to tread.

At this juncture I made my pilgrimage to Saarbrücken. In addition, two things came to my rescue and have repeatedly proven their usefulness in the classroom ever since. The second time around, I organized the course around Katharina Reiss' notion of "text typology."[1] I assume that you all enjoy at least a passing acquaintance with the way in which Reiss divides texts into those which serve an informational function, those which serve an expressive function, and those which serve an operative function. Under "informational" texts she includes all texts of an essentially factual or content-oriented nature, everything from newspaper reports and directions for the use of an appliance to scholarly or scientific literature. By "expressive" texts Reiss means poetical or literary documents whose chief purpose is to express the creativity and subjectivity of the author. Her "operative" texts, finally, are those which aim primarily to elicit a specific response in the receiver, and they comprise many forms of direct appeal from religious proselytizing or political propaganda to advertising messages.

Neither Reiss nor I regard these three classifications as "pure types" by any means: obviously, virtually all expressive or operative texts, apart perhaps from Adamitic language, Dadist poetry or the chanting of nonsense syllables, will have *some* informational component. Even in a scientific or scholarly article, we often gain some sense of the author's personal style. And the question of a writer's appeal to his or her audience, in whatever text type, is even more complex. Nevertheless, I have found it extremely enlightening and helpful for students to begin my translation course with an introduction to this system of classifying texts. Of course, "something is always lost in translation"; but if we are able to define at the outset the basic purpose which the text is intended to serve [and for simplicity's sake in the introductory course, I always assume an identity of purpose in the original German and the English translation], then it is relatively easy for us to set clear priorities. When "something" must be "lost," we are in a better position to decide what we can afford to sacrifice, and what must be retained at all costs.

Thus in an informational text, accuracy of factual information and ease of comprehension are paramount; the idiosyncrasies of an individual author's style become clearly secondary. In an expressive text, however, style acquires far greater significance, and the translator must attempt to reproduce in the target language not just the literal meaning of the text but the connotations and associations, the rhythm and cadence of the original as well. The structural network of the original, its moods, images and motifs as well as twists of plot and quirks of character, must be conveyed as sensitively and consistently as possible. Not surprisingly, the students who translate literature most successfully are generally my most sophisticated readers of literature. An operative text, finally, is supposed to move the receiver to a particular behavior. It can only do so, however, if the text makes an appropriate appeal or "strikes the right chord." Which chord is the "right" one? The answer is largely contingent upon the cultural background of the receiver and on barely conscious associations. For example, to convey the notion of "staple of life" in a translation of the Lord's Prayer intended for Eskimos, Reiss cites "Give us this day our daily fish."[2]

I acquaint my students, in order of increasing difficulty, with informational, expressive and operative texts. I consider it essential, in the interest of a thorough and complete introduction to translation, that they understand the unique challenge posed by each text type; and that they at least try their hand at each. Thus literary translation has a firm place in my curriculum. Because of the great variety of informational texts, their relative ease of translation and the practical usefulness of this type of translation, about 60% of our translations are of informational texts; about 20% are expressive texts and the remaining 20% are operative texts. Another way to describe this would be to say that we progress from the micro-textual to the macro-textual and finally to the meta-textual.

The other source for basic guidelines, this time of a slightly less general nature, was Wolf Friederich's *Technik des Übersetzens, Englisch und Deutsch*.[3] In this extraordinary little collection of contrastive examples, Friederich suggests that German tends toward a more abstract, implicit, impersonal and nominal mode of expression, whereas idiomatic English requires more concrete, explicit, personal and verbal formulations. I shared many of Friederich's examples with my class but remained skeptical at first about making a general rule out of the tendencies he had observed. Repeatedly, however, in the course of the semester, when a formulation was technically irreproachable but just didn't "sound English," we found we could make it vastly better by changing to a personal subject, by turning a noun into a verb or adding just a little more explicit information.

Along with Reiss' and Friederich's general guidelines, I used some exercises in levels of style in English and German to sensitize students to this aspect of their source and target languages. First I gave them "ranking" exercises: students received a sheet with groups of roughly synonymous words or phrases, in English or in German, and they were expected to rank each item in a group of three or four synonyms according to whether it represented an "elevated," "standard," "colloquial" or "slang" level of speech. Then, as a follow-up to the German rankings, students were asked to translate the words or phrases into their English equivalents —

equivalents, it goes without saying, in level of style as well as in meaning. In a different kind of style exercise, I produced a list of fairly colorless German expressions and sentences — "Wie geht es Ihnen?" or "Guten Tag" or "Ich bin müde," "Sie möchte gehen" or "Er hat kein Geld" — and we simply brainstormed to see how many different English formulations we could come up with along the entire style spectrum.

Students generally enjoyed these exercises a great deal, apart from learning something, and that proved not only pleasant for all of us but also important for our rapport as work progressed into more difficult and less amusing areas. For I might add parenthetically that a problem arose between my students and me that I had not encountered before. It was the issue of their command of the English language — or their lack of it. While students were quite accustomed to accept criticism of their German from me, they were distinctly reluctant to admit their English could be flawed; it was, after all, their mother tongue. Dealing appropriately with this problem required sensitivity on my part and much good will on theirs.

But even with Reiss and Friederich and exercises in levels of style, we did not feel entirely prepared to follow through the "decision-making process" of translation as Jirí Lewy described it.[4] Lewy saw the translation process, in simple terms, as one in which the translator begins with a set of possible choices or a paradigm. Each successive choice, based on a successive criterion which the translation must fulfill, narrows the field of possible choices until the translator has arrived, ideally, at the single, optimal target language equivalent.

Now, making choices is difficult enough. But I would submit that the student who is just learning to translate has an even more basic problem. And that is *having* a reasonably large field of possible equivalents to choose *from*. Indeed, how many of us, faced with a paradigm of 6 or 8 lexical choices, have not wished there were just one more member in the group, the "right" one! Clearly, students need to cultivate the ability to see possibilities for modification or adaption; they must expand their active repertoire of vocabulary,

syntactic constructions, idioms, proverbs, allusions, cultural associations and levels of style. A good translator must have the kind
of mental flexibility which suggests to him or her a variety of
possible renderings and thus creates the necessary precondition for
choosing the optimal rendering. A student who clings slavishly to
the diction of the original text, who creates neologisms or offends
against standard syntax or normal word order in the target language, clearly does not possess this kind of flexibility: the ability
to run a phrase or clause through a variety of semantic and syntactic permutations. First students must acquire this linguistic agility,
it seemed to me; only afterward could we apply such general
guidelines as Reiss' or Friederich's to help students develop the
discrimination and judgement to choose, in each case, the most
satisfactory equivalent.

Clearly, then, my job was twofold: I had to make students aware
of the choices they had, and then I must help them in each case to
make the very best possible choice. I realized that Reiss and Friederich provided valuable help in this second phase, but where was
I to look for help with the more basic first phase?

Well, clearly anyone who owns a bilingual dictionary has at hand
a major aid in finding semantic correspondences. But just as clearly
it can't solve all a translator's problems. What was one to do about
syntactic divergencies? Or about divergencies which had both a
semantic and a syntactic element? That was when I got the second
great shock of my career as a teacher of translation. I apparently
have led a very sheltered life. In any case, to my boundless amazement and dismay, there was no straightforward contrastive grammar of English and German available to which I could resort, no
comparative stylistics of German and English such as was produced for French in the thirties. There was nothing for it but to take
on the dragon myself.

What I have done since by no means claims to be an exhaustive
comparison of German and English. It is based upon lists of high-
frequency German vocabulary and expressions,[5] and it is primitive
and crude in the extreme. But at the very least it allows me to

survey with students some of the basic points of convergence and divergence in this language pair. For each point I have produced a brief discussion of the problem, followed by examples and exercises for the student to complete.

Sometimes my discussions and exercises have emphasized semantic equivalence, sometimes syntactic equivalence, and sometimes the interplay between them. For example, when we compared prepositions in German and English, we found that some were very nearly semantic equivalents; "hinter," for example, or "zwischen." Others, like "bei," had a field of meaning which was vastly different from any single English equivalent and which therefore needed to be rendered by a whole variety of possible English alternatives, depending upon context. Because of their historical relationship, English and German also possess large areas of syntactic equivalence; but there were also instances, for example in the case of extended adjective constructions, anticipatory constructions or passive subjectless sentences, where English simply has nothing similar. These were in fact the first "trouble spots" I had instinctively tried to attack. They proved relatively easy to teach because the structures are so unique and easily diagnosed that students feel comfortable translating them "freely."

Most difficult and most confusing for students were near-equivalents (for example, the use of English impersonal "it" to begin some sentences, but not nearly as many different kinds of sentences as in the German) and cases of interplay between syntactic and semantic elements. By "interplay" I mean, for example, a situation in which an exact syntactic equivalent *exists* in the target language, but where standard usage in the target language *prefers* a different syntactic structure in order to get the equivalent source language message across on an equivalent level of style. Since structure must serve meaning and purpose of the text, I taught that we must subordinate structure to meaning and choose the semantic/stylistic rather than syntactic equivalent in such a situation. Seeing, and when appropriate choosing, such syntactic alternatives, is a good part of that mental flexibility I mentioned earlier.

As an example, we can take the German expression "die Absicht haben" versus the English "to intend." Now clearly, a similar construction is possible in English: one can "have an intention," though the verb-plus-noun structure is more likely when it undergoes the negative transformation and we say we have "no intention." In English, the positive equivalent of German "die Absicht haben" is the active verb "to intend." This is simply the preference of standard usage. Of course, German does have an active verb, too: "beabsichtigen." But this belongs to a slightly higher level of style than the nominal formulation. Similarly German uses a reflexive verb, "sich freuen," where almost the same syntactic construction is possible in English — "to rejoice" — but where normal usage dictates that the optimal equivalent is "to be happy" or "to be glad." In German, conversely, the infinitive "sein" plus the adjective "froh" is also possible, but not quite as common as the active reflexive verb.

Now, I don't mean to belabor the obvious for an expert audience. But my point is that for students just beginning to translate, this is not at all obvious. They need to know what are the allowable, even mandatory, departures from the word-for-word translations they produced in first- or second-year German, they need some rules of thumb for when to use which, and they need some drills which allow them to apply what they've learned. This is what I have tried to accomplish with my contrastive exercises. I do not claim scientific rigor or all-inclusiveness for my explanations, and I do not claim to have come up with every conceivable way that the modal "wollen" or the impersonal pronoun "man" can be translated. But I would hope that we had dealt in this way with perhaps a good 80% of the situations a beginning translator is likely to run into.

And this is how I got into the business of writing a textbook. When I first started asking "Would you like to publish mine?" the question lay somewhere between a joke and a dare. But over the years I have acquired such a volume of materials that I thought I ought to do something useful with them. It seems to me that a student who wishes to study translation, in the first year at least, can do well with a simple, well-organized textbook which systematically discusses significant points of similarity and divergence between German and English, provides plentiful exercises aimed at developing facility in specific kinds of transfers, and then allows the student to apply that facility in translating a carefully selected prose passage.

As I said before, in my own course informational texts occupy about 60% of our time, expressive texts another 20% and operative texts the remaining 20% or so. Informational texts are a good place to begin because they allow us to deal in relative isolation with semantic or syntactic problems. A mail order catalogue, for example, will provide merchandise descriptions which in their brevity present virtually no grammatical problems at all, while making considerable demands on the student's knowledge of the specialized vocabulary of, say, fashion or sporting goods. When I give an assignment of this kind, I always suggest that students examine the descriptions of similar goods in a Sears or Montgomery Ward catalogue, since a normal bilingual dictionary is simply not equal to the task. A scholarly article, on the other hand, may present staggering syntactic complexities; its vocabulary, however, in spite of its apparent difficulty, is readily accessible to other specialists in the field who are familiar with the technical cognates in their native tongues. Here I try to match my assignments to the sciences my students have already studied, most frequently psychology and biology. Business letters, an interview, the directions for preparing a packet of dried soup — all provide practice in the semantic and syntactic idioms peculiar to these "sub-genres" of the informational text.

After exposing students to a fairly wide and representative range of informational texts and at the same time subjecting them to the contrastive drills I have described, it is time to make the transition to expressive texts. Here I differ with Reiss in that I include a far wider range of pre- and sub-literary texts under this heading: personal letters, diaries, certain kinds of magazine or newspaper articles, literary short forms and other items. I submit that this approach is not only theoretically justified but pedagogically useful as well; for if we define "expressive" texts in this way, we are able to introduce students gradually to the challenges of the literary text. Pre- or sub-literary texts provide excellent examples of conscious manipulation of form and content, of imagery, style and rhetorical devices, for the purpose of personal expression. But if the true artist is an innovator or creator, then the "pre-artist" is a skilled user of forms and conventions already available in the given cultural milieu; and a student, naturally enough, is more likely to have ready access to these existing devices. When students begin to translate the "formbetont" or expressive text, these pre-literary works offer a place where they can find a toehold and from there develop further skill.

As we turn to expressive texts, this is also an ideal time to introduce another kind of semantic exercise. Up until this point, students have been largely concerned with the meaning, connotation, applicability and level of style of individual words. But now they can be formally introduced to idioms, sayings, proverbs, quotations and the like. In this way they begin to think in terms of larger units of meaning which must be translated not literally but in terms of an equivalent image, standard saying or proverbial expression — or failing that, the meaning of the original will have to be paraphrased. In my drills I certianly do not attempt to expose my students to every colorful expression or word of wisdom in the German language. But we do hammer away at this kind of problem long enough so that they recognize such a unit when they come across it — even if they do not immediately understand it — and know how it must be treated.

One area in which students are likely to have a sizable repertoire of such expressions is the colloquial and slang usage of social intercourse. That is why the first expressive texts I assign are generally personal letters and social conversations. They provide an area of translation where, once students get the hang of it, they can put their knowledge to work with gratifying results. Building on that, similar scenes can be chosen for translation from a a variety of authors; in a beginning course, however, I think it prudent to limit my choices to the 20th century and to avoid dialect or other counter-productive complexities. I have xeroxed two rather challenging but instructive texts which I have also assigned: Margot Schroeder's "Seine Firma heißt Familie" and Irmtraud Morgner's "Kaffee verkehrt." Both are relatively short passages, which I find advantageous because it enables students who are perhaps not very literary in their inclinations to get a sense of the unity of content and form, of wholeness, and of the importance of a sustaining consistency in the translation of a piece. The Schroeder piece takes the language of business and the business letter, language which we used to translate business letters earlier in the course, and turns it into the image which sustains her satire with such scathing irony. Morgner's "Kaffee verkehrt" protrays an old game, the eternal pastime of sexual pursuit, but this time with a male/-female role reversal. The very title becomes a pun on the traditional relationship between the sexes, and Morgner relentlessly pursues this reversal through a whole series of delicious images to the final punch line.

Operative texts, finally, have proven most challenging, not only to translate but to select in the first place. Advertisements and advertising gimmicks such as contests have lent themselves most easily to the purposes of my course. In preparatory discussions of the translation passage, we have had to consider not only the syntax and vocabulary most appropriate to the context or the demands of rhyme and rhythm in a jingle; we have also had to reflect on the class, psychology and cultural biases of a German versus an American audience. At times, after studying the German advertisement and comparing it with ads for similar items in the US, we even realized that to be most effective in the US, the advertisement should probably be entirely rewritten. At such times we found ourselves quite literally at the edge of the untranslatable, and that in itself was instructive.

I generally assign one translation per week, in addition to the exercises and "research missions" I have already described. When students have handed in their translations, I prepare a synopsis of their results. Looking over their work, I determine which sentences or phrases have either caused particular difficulties or led to particularly interesting translations. I then type out these sentences, in order of their appearance in the text, and beneath each one I list the students' "answers" — not just the possible "right" answers, I should like to emphasize, but almost *all* the answers, within limits, and in particular "wrong" ones. This is a technique I learned in Saarbrücken and adapted slightly to suit my purposes. Of course it does mean quite a lot of work, but I consider such a synopsis indispensable to an intelligent discussion of the translation. In my translation textbook I hope to include ditto masters with a breakdown of translation passages, various renderings, room for the instructor to add examples from his or her own class, and brief notes on the merits or failings of the alternatives.

When the synopsis is distributed in class, students not only hear about but are able to see before them a whole range of alternative renderings. During the discussion which follows, we are able to criticize or defend those alternatives with complete candor, for their authors remain anonymous. We are sometimes able to synthesize an optimal equivalent out of the good ideas contained in several versions. And at the very least, when a rendering must be rejected, the student learns *why* it must be rejected and need not feel like a victim of professorial arbitrariness.

With the aid of the synopsis, we examine the translation we have produced, comparing, eliminating, refining and attempting to reach some sort of consensus. We try to apply everything we have learned up to that point, from general principles like Reiss' "text types" and Friederich's contrastive guidelines through specific techniques for dealing with problems of syntax, semantics or style. Thus the discussion becomes an occasion for recapitulation and a mutual testing: a testing both of the translation and of the principles and techniques by which we have arrived at it. I do hope that the publication of my textbook will serve to stimulate further that ongoing process of correction and refinement.

NOTES

1. Katharina Reiss, "Der Texttyp als Ansatzpunkt für die Lösung von Über-setzungsproblemen." *Linguistica Antwerpiensia* 7 (1973), 111-127; —, "Die Bedeutung von Texttyp und Textfunktion für den Übersetzungsprozeß." *Linguistica Antwerpiensia* 5 (1971), 137-147; —, *Möglichkeiten und Grenzen der Übersetzungskritik. Kategorien und Kriterien für eine sachgerechte Beurteilung von Übersetzungen.* Munich, 1971; —, "Das Problem der Textklassifikation in angewandt- linguistischer Sicht." *Linguistica Antwerpiensia* 8 (1974), 43-60.

2. Katharina Reiss, "Der Texttyp," p. 111.

3. Wolf Friederich, *Technik des Übersetzens. Deutsch und Englisch.* Munich, 1979.

4. Jiri Lewy, *"Translation as a Decision Process."* In: *To Honor Roman Jakobson,* vol. 2. The Hague, Paris, 1967, 1171-1182.

5. J. Alan Pfeffer, *Grunddeutsch. Basic (Spoken) German Dictionary.* Englewood Cliffs, NJ, 1970. *Das Zertifikat Deutsch als Fremdsprache,* ed. by Deutscher Volkshochschulverband and Goethe-Institut. Munich, 1977.

Dimension

A Literary Anomaly

A. Leslie Willson
University of Texas

The topic of this address is the *Wirkungsgeschichte*, the history of the impact, of a literary magazine that was conceived some twenty-three years ago and that first saw the light of day in June, 1968. *Dimension*, a literary oddity, incongruously edited and published deep in the heart of Texas — incongruously, because its focus is not legendary outlaws west of the Pecos and longhorn sagas but rather is the contemporary writing of German-language countries, and one would expect its site of publication to be Munich or Cologne or Hamburg or Berlin or Vienna or Zurich, not Austin, Texas — this literary anomaly grew from the editor's realization in about 1965 that much, if not most, of the literary translations from German were (and regrettably too often still are) execrably done, even fraudulently done, and from his despair over the time-block that existed (and to an extent still exists) between the date on which a work appeared abroad and the date, months or years later, when American readers and critics became aware of it. *Dimension* has always sought assiduously to redress those two immense shortcomings: the lack of quality translations and the lagging information. In words I wrote for the premiere announcement of the magazine:

> Dimension . . . hopes to bridge the deplorable cultural time lag be-
> tween the United States and Germany, a lag which exists at a mo-
> ment when creative ideas and the exchange of literary experience
> should be swifter than space-age jetaircraft. Trends in the arts and in
> literature, experimentation in stagecraft, rumblings in the literary
> and artistic avantgarde, the spirited engagement of modern writers
> in human affairs today will affect tomorrow's writers.
> Unfortunately, such stirrings become known to American readers
> and critics only through the specialized mediation of academic
> criticism or through years of slow accretion of publicity and even-
> tual translation. *Dimension* will try to make the experience of litera-
> ture in German-speaking lands immediate and vital."

Because the editor did not want the magazine to become known
under the rubric of "quarterly," it began, and continues, to appear
three times a year. The eclectic, pluralistic persuasion of the editor
was stated in the first "Perspective" page (a regular feature of
Dimension) by the then-advisory editor, Helmut Rehder, who wrote
under the title of "By Way of Welcome":

> It is the purpose of this periodical to acquaint the inquisitive with
> the newest and most striking manifestations of poetic and literary
> creativeness in Germany without being partial to any particular
> direction or doctrine, scheme or school. . . . The pages of this journal
> aim to inform rather than persuade. . . . Observing the present with
> an eye to the future will enable *Dimension* to achieve its purpose —
> the purpose of being a forum for poet-watchers on the contem-
> porary scene in Germany and a gauge for the enduring substance
> and symbols of modern thought.

The initial conception of *Dimension* turned out to be more modest
than the actuality: The magazine was proposed as having less than
100 pages per issue, published at a cost of about $4000 annually.
As it turned out, the issues have averaged 200 pages and the
monies — which pay the printer, very modest fees to authors, and
take care of postage and office supplies — now amount to more
than $20,000. In the early years the Graduate School of The Univer-
sity of Texas at Austin, under the leadership of Dean Gordon
Whaley, set aside $5,000 per annum to support *Dimension*. In 1975,
however, with a new dean and new guidelines for financial support

of magazines, the funds were moved to the University of Texas Press and *Dimension* — because the editor refused firmly to compromise with format, quality paper, and a reduction in size — was left essentially reliant only on subscription income. The editor's appeal for funds was answered by the Federal Republic of Germany which, through its international cultural agency Inter Nationes, subscribed for 300 copies, a subscription subsidy that has kept the magazine afloat. And the editor has never received the slightest indication of untoward editorial influence from the Federal Republic of Germany — else he would immediately cancel the arrangement. The subscription price more than tripled in twenty-two years — from $6 to $20 annually for individuals. The title and format was determined in advance of the first issue, naturally.

The title *Dimension* is not accidental. The editor listed about twenty possible names for the magazine, then researched existent journals for duplication, and settled finally on *Dimension*, in part because it defined, albeit vaguely and even ambiguously, what he had in mind, but also because it was by its nature bilingual. To his amazement and amusement it has turned out that the German equivalent, *Dimension*, is almost studiously ignored by German-speaking readers and contributors to the magazine, who persist in calling the magazine by its American vacables: *Dimension*.

In the color of their jackets the three issues of *Dimension* were meant to reflect approximately the color of the seasons in which they appeared: an icy, wintry blue for the first issue; a sunny, warmly hued bright yellow for the second in summer; and a ruddy, roseate glow for the third in the autumn. The fresh green of springtime is missing — that color was to be reserved for special issues — however, it happened that a less seasonal color was chosen, nonreferential white. There have been four special issues: a Günter Grass symposium issue of 1970; an East-German issue of 1973, guest-edited by Günter Kunert; a Dutch issue of 1978, guest-edited by Francis Bulhof; and in 1983 an issue celebrating 300 years of German-American relation, "The Image of America in Contemporary German Writing," 570 pages long, guest edited by Fred

Viebahn. The sequence of color remains, as does the Times Roman typeface and the design of the bilingual facing pages. From the first issue, original and unpublished contributions in German were signaled by the *Dimension* trademark, a triform, deltoid triangle.

The content format of *Dimension* has remained stable. The magazine's editorial page is "Perspective," which has presented remarks on literary trends, genres, and translation by various authors and critics. It was for several years followed by a literary letter in English, usually translated (but Ernst Jandl sent his from Vienna in English), and usually from Germany, though occasionally from elsewhere, which summed up the most recent publications in the realm of literature or which may address a specific genre or trend. The letter was discontinued some years ago. The literary texts that then follow always appear in German and in facing-page English translations. In arranging the contents the editor has chosen to emphasize the first, the middle, and the end of each issue with works he feels are outstanding, except in those instances where the number of contributors and the element of an issue focused on a specific area (East Germany) or topic (children's literature), when the contents have been arranged alphabetically by author. There have been double issues that featured the literature of Austria and German-speaking Switzerland. Following the literary texts come "Authors and Translators," which lists contributors incondensed bibliographical paragraphs. The last issue of each volume contains an index to that volume. A five-year index is in the final issue of volume five and a ten-year, expanded index in the final issue of volume ten. After the appearance of volume twenty a twenty-year index will be published separately.

From the beginning *Dimension* attracted notice. Mathias Schreiber, in the *Kultur-Magazin* of the *Neue Presse am Sonntag* on 22 December 1968, wrote that *Dimension* was "an elegant magazine for contemporary German literature. In appearance and contents *Dimension* is multi-dimensional, lively, carefully printed and edited." In January 1969 the *Times Literary Supplement* wrote in regard to *Dimension*: "For once 'contemporary' is justified. . . . Refreshing emphasis on literature rather than criticism." In March 1969 the *Deutsche Welle*, in comments written by Hans Bender, broadcast that "*Dimension*'s appearance and open-minded character are momentous." Also in March *The Library Journal* called *Dimension* "an outstanding journal of current German thought. " The first reviews were in, and the enterprise seemed to be successfully launched. A year later Horst Bienek, in the *Frankfurter Allgemeine Zeitung*, remarked that *Dimension* was "personal, spontaneous, undoctrinary" and that it published "new works not known even in Germany. " You can imagine the editor's pleasure at reading: "Information about what our authors are presently writing is more entertaining and more inclusive than all the literary pages of our cultural magazines put together." And finally Bienek summed up his impression with the words: "Unaffected, informative, objective, topical." Finally, in the fall of 1970, *The Saturday Review* mentioned that *Dimension* had "won the high regard of elite European literary circles." The magazine was on its way.

 Dimension is still on its way, even though it may be , as Horst Bienek suggested in his review, that it "could almost be called a paradox." Bienek was impressed that *Dimension*, edited and published in Texas, had begun to function as a kind of preview of things to come in German letters, through the publication particularly of previously unpublished work by German writers. He mentions Peter Bichsel's "A Table is a Table," which appeared in *Dimension* two years before its publication in a collection of tales abroad; Uwe Johnson's essay on New York appeared in *Dimension* in the summer of 1968, though even now official bibliographies list its first appearance as being that in *Die Neue Rundschau* in spring 1969 (later Johnson wove it into his novel, *Jahrestage*). Bienek mentions the opening chapter of a novel by Martin Gregor-Dellin, a story by Günter Kunert, a long poem by Heinz Piontek, a radio play by Wolfgang Weyrauch, a one-act play by Jürg Federspiel. He lists also the story by Siegfried Lenz, "The Blindfold," which the author later turned into a two-act play with the same title (for the celebratory issue of *Die Gruppe 47* in 1987 – volume 16/3 – Lenz submitted another unpublished story, "A Helping Hand.") He also cites poems by Christoph Meckel, Walter Helmut Fritz, and Bernd Jentzsch. He exults at the discovery that Wolf Wondratschek "has written a few excellent poems that far surpass his prize-winning shallow Jarry poem." What Bienek did not know was that the editor had been offered the Jarry poem, the winner of a literary prize awarded by Wolfgang Weyrauch, but had rejected it, not knowing it was the prize-winning poem.

What were the first years like? Work, of course, began months and months ahead of the appearance of an issue. Contributions had to be solicited — with great success from both well-known and little-known authors — and then they had to be translated by known and unknown translators. In this regard *Dimension* has been and continues to be a proving ground and try-out opportunity for aspiring translators, whose efforts are carefully checked by the editor before publication. Some publishers were less than cooperative, not eager to add *Dimension* to review lists — the magazine does not, after all, review books. But it does reprint from books. But now that situation has been completely reversed. *Dimension* now receives most contemporary contributions directly from leading German publishers, though there are still a few hold-outs such as the Austrian *Residenz Verlag*, and from authors directly. The worst experience by the editor in the first years was that of the arrogance of agents, with that of those few American agents for those few German publishers who employ agents. In some instances the editor had to appeal directly to the author (once to Hans Erich Nossack and once to Hubert Fichte) because the self-seeking and perhaps over-protective agents adamantly refused to permit works to appear in *Dimension* or else insisted on fees the magazine was unable to pay in competition with *Playboy* (cited by one agent, though subsequently the author involved never appeared in *Playboy*, and the work involved never appeared in English at all). Heinrich Böll, although repeatedly willing, remained unrepresented to his death because of his agent's firm naysaying.

But as *Dimension* continued to appear, continued to introduce authors to English readers (and even to German readers), the editor's mailbox began to contain unsolicited manuscripts from authors, both from those established and form those still relatively unknown, from both Germanies, Austria, Switzerland, and from elsewhere — from Scandinavia and from Czechoslovakia and Rumania. My first searches for new authors often included the *Times Literary Supplement* reviews and those in various German newspapers. In the *TLS* I read a review of the first book of poetry by a German engineer. Intrigued, I wrote him via the publisher and subsequently published Fritz von Opel's memorial to Erich Maria Remarque, "Were We Not, What We Are." Little did I know when I first wrote to him, that he was the same Opel of the automotive works and jet-propulsion pioneering, since 1933 retired and living in Switzerland. In *Die Welt* on 25 April 1968 I read the review of a first book of poetry by a young poet and student of German literature, then twenty-two years old. The reviewer wrote: "The sole talent of the author seems to be his ability to make involuntary bad puns." Since my own puns are invariably involuntary and usually bad, I felt a certain kind of kinship with young Frank Geerk, so I wrote him, inviting a contribution to *Dimension*, reserving my editorial right to make up my own mind about the quality of his work and citing the source of my interest, the negative review. In his reply to my query, Geerk wrote that he found it was "marvelous" that my attention to him had been drawn by a vicious review of his first book. Subsequently I published prose and poems by Geerk, conincidentally in an issue that contained epigrams by Elias Canetti. Not until years later did I learn that, upon the appearance of the issue, Canetti — a resident of Switzerland — had contacted Geerk in Basel and had become his literary advocate and his friend. Today Frank Geerk, who was a visiting writer at the University of Texas at Austin in the spring of 1980, is a playwright, poet, and novelist, who has just finished a long novel, the action of which takes place mainly in the American Southwest, a novel that he calls a twentieth-century *Heinrich von Ofterdingen* in reverse.

Occasionally I have, as you might imagine, encountered thorny problems in translation, both in my own efforts and in those of other translators whom I check constantly. One such problem arose with a text by Hubert Fichte, in which two words occurred whose meaning I intuited but wished to verify incontrovertibly. The words were: "Aderflügler" and "Schwurgift." The first was, I decided, those insects whose wings reveal visible vein structure — and Fichte confirmed that guess, so I translated the word as hymenoptera, a species of insects that includes flies, bees, and the like. The second word, a neologism, proved more problematical. I sought the assistance of a genial reference librarian at the University of Texas, asking her to search out a possible ritual that involved the drinking of poison on the occasion of oath-taking. She reported to me that my request had made her an authority both on poisons and on oath-taking, but she had been unable to discover a specific term that related to such a ceremony. She had, however, assembled a few books for me to consult. In those I discovered first that an African tribe had such a ceremony, whereby a witness drank poison as a proof of veracity in testimony. And second, the often-seen Greek oath "By the Styx!" became clear to me, for the River Styx is a poisonous river and could well serve as the source of the poison-proven oath. I would have preferred to translate "Schwurgift," therefore, as Stygian potion, but since no reference to Greek lore occurred in Fichte's work, that choice was not a viable one, for it would have introduced an alien element into the narrative. Therefore I compromised with "ordeal by poisonous potion," a lame effort admittedly. Fichte, to whom I reported the results of my research, wrote in reply: "Schwurgift is indeed a neologism of mine. Your remarkable thoroughness would have moved me to admit Greek components throughout my book. . . . Xango and a certain Zeus are both androgynous, both are gods of lightning, and the attribute of both is the two-headed ax."

Such an exchange with an author has not been rare in the editorial office of *Dimension*. I once felt obliged to query Gabriele Wohmann in regard to a poem in which she described a cocktail party and the relative positions of various celebrants — and it turned out, she had indeed erred. In answer to my query she wrote: "You are very exact, I'm inexact. I made myself a sketch, but suddenly no longer knew at all by whom the man was standing and what was left or right of him. . . . Surely the change of climate between Rome and Darmstadt is to blame . . . (one always looks for an excuse)."

Another instance of a specific connection between the *Dimension* editorial office and the work of a writer occurred with a story submitted by Friederike Mayröcker. She sent *In einer verfallenen Nachbarschaft*, which I read with great interest and slowly dawning understanding — and also with some puzzlement, since many phrases and incidents in the narrative were quite familiar to me. When I looked into our previous correspondence, I discovered that Mayröcker had not only incorporated into the story incidents I had described to her but that she had even used my own words verbatim, with repeated introductory insertions of "sagte er." I understood then why, on the manuscript, she had dedicated the narrative to me. I can only surmise that much of the story also contained verbatim quotations from letters written to her by Ernst Jandl, who happened to be at the University of Texas as a visiting writer at the time. From my report to her that roses bloom in December in Austin, she had put together a narrative that included references to the French Quarter in New Orleans (visited by Jandl), a narrative about the winter or life and the promise that late blossoms bring.

One aspect of the purpose of *Dimension*, the improvement of literary translation into English from German, has been adhered to tenaciously. Every manuscript translation is checked thoroughly, followed by a written consultation with the translator before the manuscript is released for publication. The editor has solicited translations from 196 translators: from undergraduate and graduate students, from colleagues in Austin and elsewhere around the world, and from professional translators in America and abroad. All translators, whatever their experience or status, have been treated equally in editorial matters. Errors and infelicities have been pointed out and questions of interpretations discussed at length. The translation mode preferred by the editor is one that tries to reproduce the original as faithfully as possible, both in regard to content as well as to style and author's intention. The wide spectrum of styles and genres has required the most resourceful application of effort by translators, both by those experienced in the craft as well as by those in effect appreticing themselves through the editorial office of *Dimension*. The editor has returned repeatedly to those translators who have proven to be equal to the tasks assigned to them. Occasionally the editorial repair work necessary to turn a pallid translation into a palatable one has been so extensive that the editor has felt it necessary to inquire of the translator whether credit should be extended. Generally the translator has pleaded in such instances that credit should be extended. The editor has followed the preference of the translator, who, however, was never asked to translate for *Dimension* again.

Any translator, whatever his or her expertise and experience, can make an error, either of interpretation or of lexigraphical, semantic, or grammatical reading. Whether the error be produced by haste, unfamiliarity with a style or an allusion, or be simple ignorance, no translator is exempt from falling victim to a lapse of attention or a careless misreading or to the connotations of an exotic allusion. Overzealousness can contribute to mistakes as well. The most embarrassing mistake perpetrated by the editor was in regard to a work by Ernst Jandl, known to the editor only through its title. In the "Authors and Translators" section of *Dimension*, which has become a standard source of reference for readers and critics, titles of works by featured authors are mentioned and given also in parenthetical translation. In an early issue of *Dimension*, in which Ernst Jandl appeared for the first time, reference was made to a slim edition of a work published in 1965 by the Writer's Forum, *Poets*, in London. The title of the work was: *mai hart lieb zapfen eibe hold*, a series of unrelated words, viewed semantically. Knowing the propensity of Jandl for experimental, superficially nonsensical poetry, the editor, in compiling the entry for "Authors and Translators," translated the title as: *may hard dear taps yew lovely*, not knowing that he had fallen into a treacherous trap. Only later did he discover, both to his consternation and to his immense amusement, that he had falsely translated the first line of a Jandl poem that bears the title: "Oberflächliche Übersetzung" — Superficial Translation. The work is perhaps familiar to some of you. If not, then perhaps the original, to which Jandl gave a daring and original translation, may be familiar to you. The German "mai hart lieb zapfen eibe hold" is a superficial translation of the first line of the Wordsworth poem that begins: "My heart leaps up when I behold /a rainbow in the sky."

In the third issue of volume seven of *Dimension* may be found the earliest poems selected by Paul Celan for publication, poems that never appeared because he had the first volume of his poetry destroyed in 1948, ostensibly because of an inordinate number of typographical errors. In 1967 Robert de Beaugrande met Celan in Paris and was given copies of those earliest seventeen poems, gathered together under the title of "At the Gates" and omitted from Celan's *Mohn und Gedächtnis*. They never received public circulation before their appearance in 1974 in *Dimension*, in the original German and in translation by de Beaugrande. Even today they have not yet appeared in the collected poetry of Celan in the Suhrkamp edition of his writing. They appear in *Dimension*.

Though the editing of *Dimension* has amounted to an intensive and unremitting task, the editor has enjoyed bonuses. The contributions of artists has enriched his walls — prints by HAP Grieshaber, Alex Hertenstein, Günter Bruno Fuchs; etchings by Joachim Braatz, Christoph Meckel, and Karlheinz Pilcz; watercolors by Erich Fitzbauer, drawings by Gunter Kunert, and collages by Peter Weiss. The first issue of volume 13 (1980) — delayed by *Dimension*'s exquisite but slow printer — will contain literary and artistic contributions by twenty contemporary doubly-talented writer/artists from East and West Germany, Austria, and Switzerland, ranging from Friedrich Dürrenmatt to Peter Weiss. Further bonuses consist of books personally inscribed by authors to the editor, such as that volume received from Uwe Johnson that bore the inscription: "Hoping that you would like to know the circumstances of my death." Another bonus is the voluminous correspondence with authors, and not least the personal acquaintance of a great many of the 299 authors published in *Dimension* since 1968.

It gives me some satisfaction that *Dimension*, which in one respect has become a small part of world literature in a literal sense, seems to be responsible for a growing interest in German-language literature not only by fellow-Germanists but also by students and general readers in the English-speaking world and in Germany itself. It has become a veritable sourcebook for contemporary German writing. Its poems, stories, novel excerpts, dramas, and radio plays have been copied by innumerable classroom teachers for the benefit of students of German literature and language. It has been used as a textbook in classes that specifically focus on contemporary German writing. Various contributions have been republished in anthologies and textbooks. *Dimension* is well on its way to becoming a five-foot shelf of contemporary German literature, in the original and in translation. Issues have included the aforementioned author/graphic artists issue; a double issue on lyric poetry; a Yiddish issue; an issue devoted to previously unpublished poems; an issue that features the opening pages of untranslated novels; one that heralds German text written in non-German-speaking countries around the world, guest edited by Peter Pabisch (following an issue that features German texts written by Americans and Canadians, guest edited by Irmgard Elsner Hunt); the aforementioned issue on *Die Gruppe 47*; an issue of short stories (with a surprise revelation by Günter Grass); and an issue celebrating forty years of the Eremiten-Presse Verlag in Düsseldorf. Coming still are issues devoted to *Liedermacher*, the events of November 1989 in Germany, and texts read at the meeting of the Group 47 in Prague of spring, 1990. No doubt there are many influences exerted by the magazine that I have no knowledge of, though I have often surmised a few: such as the increasing attention paid to women writers published in the magazine; the sudden focus on the writing of East Germany after the issue edited by Gunter Kunert; specific writers presented first in *Dimension* who now find placement in other magazines and even with New York's recalcitrant publishers.

In an effort to extend even further its sphere of influence and realm of missionary fervor, *Dimension* exists also in book form in *DIMENSION: A Reader of German Literature since 1968*, a volume published in 1981 by Continuum Books under the leadership of Werner Mark Linz. The 312-page book is a reader in English only, which features a selection of works by fifty-one authors considered by the editor to be most representative, works culled from some 7000 pages of thirty-three issues of *Dimension*.

When, in the early 1980s, delays and costs in the University of Texas Printing Division became disruptive and prohibitive, the editor turned to computer production of the magazine. After doing the huge America issue and a double issue on poetry with a PC – which involved extensive coding, use of a modem, and pasting up issues on boards – the vast possibilities of desk-top publishing with the use of a MacIntosh Plus and a LaserWriter Plus changed the life of the editor, who then became a typesetter and designer as well as editor. Beginning with volume 15/2, all the issues of *Dimension* have been produced in the editor's study, even many of the covers (all those of volume 18). The format and appearance of the magazine was not changed. The contents remain various and sundry, with special attention to special trends in literary production in the German language. I hope that *Dimension* will continue to be the "showcase of modern German literature in the United States," as the back cover of *A Dimension Reader* claims.

Modern German Literature in England

A Personal Account

Michael Hamburger
United Kingdom

I must begin by making clear that I have never concerned myself with what the Germans call *Wirkungsgeschichte* or *Rezeptionsgeschichte*, a discipline calling for minute research and statistics, as well as for an approach more sociological than literary. That is my only reason for confining myself here to immediate experience gathered in the course of five decades as a translator and critic of mainly, but not exclusively, German texts. The only statistics available to me throughout those decades were my royalty statements. Even if I could draw on these for my talk, and most of them were thrown away or burned long ago, I should not bother to do so, because I don't believe that the numbers of books sold tells us anything of significance about the lives, destinies and effectiveness of the works in question. As any author is bound to discover in the course of a working life, the inescapable fact is that we know very little about the reception and effectiveness, if any, of literary works, for the simple reason that the majority of their readers keep their responses to themselves. Published comment in the form of book reviews, critical essays and the rare reader-letter are only the visible tip of an iceberg, and much of such comment is routine showing no true response to or engagement with the work commented upon. So even if I'd kept a scrapbook of press cuttings throughout those decades, and I did not, I should not wish to base my talk on that evidence. I have no alternative, therefore, to relying on my memory here – an increasingly sieve-like memory. Yet if culture, as somebody said, is what we have forgotten, so is experience the deposit or residue left over from all we've known and done. I have now made a list, I hope more or less complete, of the things I have translated. I did that specially for the purpose of this talk. So I shall run through more or less chronologically and perhaps talk a little bit more generally about the climate of opinion and taste in those various decades.

My first book of translations came out at a most unpropitious time, in the middle of the war; it was the first book-length translation of Hölderlin to appear in English. There had previously been a little book called *Hölderlin's Madness* by David Gascoyne which contained some six or eight Hölderlin translations. These however he had done from the French (he did not know German) from Pierre Jean Jouve's French versions. He was interested in Hölderlin mainly as a precursor of Surrealism, for David Gascoyne was one of the very few British Surrealists at that time, in 1938; and Pierre Jean Jouve was mainly interested in what were regarded as the poems of Hölderlin's madness, wrongly, since the best of them were written before Hölderlin was considered by anyone to be mentally ill. It so happened that this Hölderlin translation of mine appeared in time for the Centenary of Hölderlin's death, because I had done the work mainly when I was at school, and finished it by the time I was eighteen. Its publication in 1943 coincided with the Centenary. What I remember of the reception is worth mentioning, I think, because the book appeared in the middle of the war. It presented translations of the work of a German poet, and a German poet who was scarcely known in England. I remember that at school, when I became interested in Hölderlin, my teacher, a very good modern language specialist at a fairly good school, West-minster School, was horrified that I had picked on Hölderlin, and even when I later sent to him the finished book, he wrote me an appreciative letter, asking again, "Why on earth did you pick on this crazy poet?" And in the *Oxford Book of German Verse*, which was the standard book at that time read in schools and universities, a standard anthology, there was actually part of a poem by Klopstock included under Hölderlin's name. That was the state of Hölderlin studies at the time. What was astonishing, though, is the way my book was received at that time in England. It received considerably more attention than such a book would receive now. I remember, for example, that it was reviewed in *Punch*. *Punch* is, as you know, a humorous magazine, and a British institution; but the idea that such a book could be reviewed in *Punch* is absolutely inconceivable now. And it was widely reviewed in the general press in an ignorant but friendly and interested way.

I should add that there was a very strong anti-German prejudice in Britain which had nothing to do actually with National Socialism because that prejudice arose much earlier, even before the First World War. The great period for the reception of German literature was in the Victorian era, when most of the outstanding British men of letters and women of letters (like George Eliot, e.g.) were informed about German publications, knew the language and read German books. But from about the time of the death of Carlyle, who was the great champion of German literature in Britain, there was a decline, and by the time, in the forties, I arrived on the scene, that prejudice was marked in all the avant-garde circles. Cyril Connolly for instance – the influential editor of the widely read magazine *Horizon* – later published a book on modern European literature in which not a single German author was included. The orientation was all French, and French things were regarded as smart. This had a social aspect, too. It was socially obligatory to go to Paris, because all the latest things happened in Paris. There was a kind of aura of social snobbery about anything French, which didn't apply to Germany, in spite of the fact that in the thirties, various younger British writers like Auden, Spender and Isherwood went to Germany, especially to Berlin. But Auden in fact knew very little German, and his interest in German literature really developed later. Stephen Spender had some interest, as his translations and essays show, but his knowledge of the language did not match his genuine sympathy with certain German writers. Isherwood showed little interest in the literature, as far as I know.

Nevertheless, there was something about the literary scene at that time which has disappeared in England. There was a kind of seriousness about the reception of literature. Let's say that a decency was observed, even in papers that did not specialize in the arts, so that some kind of reception was assured. That is now no longer the case. Here I must also mention an episode which bears on that period, though I have written about it in my book of memoirs. By the time the Hölderlin appeared in 1943, I was in the army; and I was just doing my infantry training in England when I received an invitation from the Poetry Society in London to give a talk and reading based on my Hölderlin translations. That was the first time I was ever asked to appear in public. I was just 19 at the time, and naturally I had not had much of a public life before that. I wrote back and said, "I'm terribly sorry, but I'm doing my infantry training." So they wrote to my Company Commander in the regiment, the Royal West Kents. I received a summons, and was marched into his office. I thought I'd committed some terrible offence. (When the sergeant major marches you in, it usually means you're to be punished.) But the Company Commander had received this letter, and said, "You will go to London and give this talk to represent the Regiment" – about a German poet in the middle of the war! In retrospect, I feel it was a wonderful thing, so typical of all the things that were really good in England at that time, many of which, I am sorry to say, have gone. So, I had to go and give my talk in that Poetry Society, which, at that time, was a very strange body. The audience consisted mainly of old ladies who were knitting socks and had never heard of Hölderlin. Incidentally, that book had a fairly wide circulation, although it was a book I am now very much ashamed of, a very juvenile work. It had an immensely long introduction that was full of completely irrelevant material. I had the feeling then that this might be my only book, because I was going into war and would probably die. So I thought I had to put everything I knew into the introduction. Amongst other things, I took up a statement that T. S. Eliot had made about Goethe, his notorious statement that Goethe dabbled in philosophy and poetry and made no great success of either, – another instance, by the way, of the anti-German prejudice I have mentioned. I questioned that dictum of Eliot's, and very much later T. S. Eliot took up this criticism of mine, taking back his statement about Goethe. This was in his address called *Goethe as Sage*, a lecture he gave on receiving the Goethe Prize in the 1950's. He quoted me as having forced him to revise his opinion. So my juvenile Introduction had made a little dent there. I still meet people even now who tell me: I read that book of yours back in the war. For example, Anthony Burgess, the novelist whom I once met in America, had read that book at the time. You don't know what happens to books, they go all over the place and get to the strangest people, and have the strangest effects on them sometimes.

There was a gap in my translating work, obviously, because I had four years as a soldier. Though in fact I was able to produce my next translation, of some of Beaudelaire's prose poems*, while I was a soldier, when I happened to be stationed in the Shetland Isles where there was absolutely nothing to do, and the soldiers just sat around in huts in this desolate landscape with the winds blowing around them, and everybody was so demoralized that there were not even parades.

My next translation was from the German again, but it was only half-literary and touched on music. It was a book of Beethoven's letters, journals and conversations. Although this work was one of the few commissions I have ever accepted, it fitted in with my own interests, because I've always been as much interested in music as in literature, and Beethoven at that time was one of my favourite composers. It also had an introduction which dealt with the ques-

---

*   Recently reissued by City Lights, San Francisco: Charles Baudelaire, *Twentry Prose Poems* (1988).

tion of music and literature, and the way that musicians think and how they express themselves. Beethoven had a very strange way of expressing himself in his letters. He was in fact in many ways as inarticulate in words as he was articulate in music. That linked up with a special concern of mine, and I later wrote other things on the subject. That Beethoven book has had a long life. In fact it's still in print now, thirty years after its first publication. Most of the attention it received, inevitably, was more musicological than literary.

In the following year, 1952, I published a little booklet of translations from Trakl, a very small selection of poems, published by a little press in Cornwall. I remember one review of it, in the *TLS*, in which Trakl was treated as a morbid Austrian minor poet. At that time nobody could see anything very remarkable about Trakl, though that changed in later years when there was some interest in Expressionism generally, and parallel movements in European literature. Most of those Trakl versions later appeared in a larger selection which received much more attention. It was published in London by Jonathan Cape and in America by Grossman.

In the next few years I was mainly preoccupied with critical work. I had meanwhile become a lecturer in German at the University of London. Since I had refused to write a dissertation or thesis for a doctorate, I was told that I had to produce a critical book which would be accepted in lieu of the higher degree. In actual fact I did not manage to finish that critical book during my three probationary years as an Assistant Lecturer and was therefore kicked out. I moved on to another university where they didn't care so much about these formalities. When it materialized, in 1957, the critical book linked up very closely with my translating: almost all the authors dealt with in this book, *Reason and Energy*, were authors whom I had translated, though some of those translations – of Novalis, Kleist and Büchner, for instance – appeared only in periodicals or were held back for much later book publications. My interest in Expressionism also began at that period, though it has always been an interest limited to specific works and authors – the initiators of the style and one later Expressionist, Gottfried Benn, some of whose poems I translated at that period.

It has to be said that throughout all these years I have never been able to assume any kind of knowledge of German literature, not even the most elementary historical knowledge. I still meet poeple who think that Hölderlin was a contemporary of Rilke's. So part of my critical activity in all that time has been simply the need to clarify what I was doing as a translator, and to create some kind of background of information that made a reception possible. That is why I never regarded my critical work as scholarly. I regarded it simply as something I had to do to make any kind of reception of my translations possible.

In the late 50's I started translating some works of Goethe, some of his poems and the play *Egmont,* which was published in a volume called *The Classic Theatre,* edited by Eric Bentley, in 1959. Some of the poems I translated were published in a paperback volume called *Great Writings of Goethe,* edited by Stephen Spender, in 1958. Goethe has never really established himself as an author in the English-speaking world, with the single exception of *Faust,* which was certainly very widely read in the 19th century and continues to be translated again and again. New translations are published, but there is a very great obstacle to the reception of Goethe: he doesn't fit into European developments, and people don't understand what he was doing. In Germany, as you know, he is treated mainly as a classical author. But the classical period was over in Europe by the time Goethe was writing. So in England he is treated as a romantic author; but then people can't understand why he was producing works like *Iphigenie,* which simply don't fit into their conception of Romanticism. I have noticed again and again that Hölderlin has established himself by now in the English-speaking world, in a way that Goethe's poems have not, which is very strange. It also has to do with the fact that what is appreciated most in our time is a kind of personal idiosyncracy which Hölderlin had to a great degree, whereas in Goethe there really is something classical in the sense that the stress falls more on the genre than on the personal manner or vision. Goethe tried his hand at virtually every genre, ranging in poetry from epic to lyric and epigram, and even within those genres he showed an astonishing diversity. This classical versatility has become almost incomprehensible in recent times. It's always writers that do something extremely personal and idiosyncratic who manage to establish themselves in literature, and also writers who have done something in their literature which had not been done in other literatures and therefore fill some kind of gap. Yet many of the things that Goethe did had been done before him in other literatures. There had been Shakespeare, for example; if there had been no Shakespeare, Goethe's plays would have had a completely different history in the English-speaking world. That applies to Schiller even more.

The next few years, from the late 50's to the early 60's, I was preoccupied with Hofmannsthal. Hofmannsthal interested me primarily as a phenomenon; in fact I see many parallels between Hofmannsthal and Goethe, because Hofmannsthal tried to do again what Goethe managed to do in his lifetime: to pull a whole culture together. Hofmannsthal's ambition again was not to think of himself as an individual, but to think of literature as an institution, and to provide a literature where he thought no literature existed. That attempt to me was very fascinating, so I spent many years concerned with Hofmannsthal, and even did some really scholarly work during that time – research into the books that Hofmannsthal had read, with his annotations. I went through his personal library, which was then in the possession of his son in London. This seemed worth doing, because Hofmannsthal had tried to read everything of importance, something which Eliot and Pound, to some extent, were also trying to do in the English-speaking world, – to set up a kind of canon of literature which was exemplary, and which every educated person ought to know. This was done out of the same feeling that the culture of Europe was falling apart, that there was such multiplicity in the modern world that you could no longer speak of a culture at all, because there was no common fund of knowledge or standards. In Hofmannsthal's case, this realization proved very dangerous, in that it led him very far to the Right, to what he called "the conservative revolution." Of course that applies equally to Eliot, and to Pound whose version of "the conservative revolution" made him a Fascist. But on the other hand it corresponds in some ways to what was being done on the Left by writers like Brecht. In fact there was a sympathy between Brecht and Hofmannsthal, in spite of the differences in their political associations. For Brecht was also trying to diminish the importance that was being placed on individuality in literature, and to create a literature that was an institution, more than something just done by one individual intent on expressing himself. It is also interesting, that Hofmannsthal was one of the first people to publish major works by Walter Benjamin, in his periodical *Neue Deutsche Beiträge*. Both from the Left and from the Right there were such attempts to pull all literature together, and to establish some kind of a public sphere, as it were, for literature, rather than this very segmented state.

During that time I edited two volumes of Hofmannsthal's work in English. The first was called *Poems and Verse Plays* and the second, *Plays and Libretti*. From the point of view of reception, this effort seems to have been a complete failure. It has been as impossible to establish Hofmannsthal as to establish Goethe in the English-speaking world. Again there are similar reasons, it seems, because Hofmannsthal's work doesn't make sense except as a whole, since anything that he did in the various genres has some place in a general scheme. Like Goethe, he tried to do something in all literary genres, as a critic as well as a poet, and again this approach has not been appreciated in the context of other literatures. The plays, for example, the larger plays in the second volume, were never put on a stage anywhere in Britain or the USA, as far as I know. Two of them were broadcast on the Third Programme of the BBC. There was a very impressive production of *Der Turm* on the radio, with very fine music composed for it, and it actually worked very well as a radio play. Willa Muir's translation of *Der Schwierige* was also done as a radio play. *Der Schwierige*, of course, is one of the most difficult plays to translate or to transfer to any social and lingusitic sphere other than its own, even though its Viennese aristocratic idiom is really a kind of artificial language based on that idiom which Hofmannsthal invented, a little in the way that John Synge invented a kind of beautiful Irish which was never spoken quite in the way it appears in his plays, a distillation of the vernacular. To render that kind of speech is a very, very difficult problem. Among the British aristocracy, for example, speech is very down to earth, rather coarse in many ways. There is no equivalence at all for this kind of precious language that was used by the Viennese aristocracy, at least in Hofmannsthal's day. One would have to go back in time to the 17th century, to the Restoration period, to find any kind of equivalent. But you can't translate a play set in the 20th century into 17th century English. It seems an almost insoluble problem, though not too long ago another translation of *Der Schwierige* was put on in Manchester quite successfully. So it can be done, though perhaps only by adapting the play rather freely, as Willa Muir's version did not.

It may well be that my translations of dramatic works – by Goethe, Büchner, Hofmannsthal, Kokoschka and others – are more literary than theatrical, and their failure to be staged may have something to do with that. Certainly my experience is that one needs not only a liking for the theatre but connections with producers and actors to make the transition from the printed page to the stage. The radio was a different matter, at least in the old days of the Third Programme of the BBC, when there were broadcasts both of German plays, rarely or never performed on the stage in the English-speaking world, and of the radio plays that were a flourishing medium, for poets especially, in the 50's and 60's. Thanks to some most enterprising producers at the BBC, Christopher Holme above all, many such radio plays were broadcast – including one by Peter Weiss and three by Günter Eich in my translation.

Returning to the printed page, I have to mention that my Hölderlin translation went through various metamorphoses, because the first was a very juvenile effort. There was a second edition, wholly recast and enlarged, in 1952, also published in the States. By that time I had also started to translate Hölderlin poems into the meters which he used, because I found after a time that you cannot translate Hölderlin into any other meter. In my first version I had used a kind of free verse with echoes of the metrical structure, but with no strict scheme of any kind. But from the second book onwards I tried to do them in the original meters. In 1961 I published a prose version of Hölderlin's poems, based on my verse translations, in a series called the *Penguin Poets*, and that book had a very wide circulation. I think it must have sold twenty or thirty thousand copies, which again was one of the things that was possible only in the 1960's. The 60's, I have to say, were an especially good time for the reception of foreign work. It was a time of breakthrough – also in regard to the once prevalent prejudice against German literature. It was also the time when readings of international poetry established themselves in Britain. There was a general loosening up of the rather often very parochial climate in England, and it looked as if all kinds of things were going to get through. It was also that time when Penguin Books launched their *European Poets* series, which introduced poets like Nelly Sachs, Enzensberger, Grass and even Celan to a really large public of readers, many of them among the younger and youngest generations. There was at that time a kind of vogue among young people to buy such books – a vogue that seems to have passed without a trace. People used to collect those *Penguin Books*, for example. Many young people, who were not in other ways particularly literary, were interested in these things. That's why it was possible to sell tens of thousands of copies of such works at that period. The Penguin Hölderlin went against my principles, because the whole series required literal translations, which I hate. I produced them, nonetheless, so as to get Hölderlin's own texts to readers who never would have bothered with my verse translations, but used my verse translations and set them out in prose with a few changes, so that if you read them carefully you can still catch some of the rhythms, concealed under the prose. Each edition of my Hölderlin versions has added new translations, as well as recasting some of the earlier ones. By the time I published the book called *Poems and Fragments*, in 1966, I had translated the greater part of the later work of Hölderlin, including also two *Empedocles* fragments and a selection from the rhymed verse of his so-called madness.

But during that period, in the 60's, I became more and more involved with the work of my German and Austrian contemporaries, and especially the work of people of roughly my own generation. I was translating by that time a good deal of their work as well as some older poets, such as Benn and Brecht. Then I translated three radio plays of Günter Eich and some of his poems, as well as poems of Enzensberger, Grass, Celan and Peter Huchel. I also became especially interested in the work of East German poets. One other West German writer of my age group is Helmut Heissenbüttel. I did a book, a selection from his work, which I called just *Texts*. That book appeared late in 1977. By that time, there had been a deterioration in the general reception of any serious work in any language whatsoever. That book passed virtually unnoticed both in Britain and the USA, where it was distributed. The only British review of it that I saw, in a Sunday paper, is typical of what is still happening now. Some young man who'd just come down from Oxford did review the book, but about half of the review was taken up by the story of how he was in a punt at Oxford, and was reading a book by Hermann Hesse, but suddenly decided he didn't like Hermann Hesse, and threw the book into the river. Then there were a few sentences about Helmut Heissenbüttel, treating him as a Communist, which he has never been, because there was a poem in that book called *The Future of Socialism* which is both clever and funny, being an indirect critique of Communism in the form of pure grammatical permutation. The reviewer had not even noticed the most striking characteristic of Heissenbüttel's work, the extent to which he grants autonomy to language itself, leaving it free to create, rather than convey, meaning.

In the earlier period, in 1963, together with Christopher Middleton, I produced a bilingual anthology called *Modern German Poetry 1910-1960*. That was a success, as far a such books can be a success. It maintained itself for some ten or fifteen years both in America and in Britain. I don't remember many of the reviews, but I do remember that they responded positively to work by the most various German poets. Just about that period, too, in the early 60's, something very strange happened in England, very characteristic of that breakthrough which I am talking about. There was a young man in London who suddenly became interested in the poems of Johannes Bobrowski. He was so keen on these poems that he set up a publishing firm simply in order to publish them. He inserted an advertisement in the *TLS*, advertising this book in order to get subscribers. He got something like four or five answers, but went ahead all the same. To everyone's astonishment, within a month or two the whole edition was sold out, and he had to reprint the book. Bobrowski had been virtually unknown in England. It may be that I had written about him before that somewhere in a periodical. The translations in question were not mine, because another translator, Matthew Mead, had translated the poems with the help of his wife Ruth. He sent his work to Bobrowski, who consulted Christopher Middelton and me, and we decided that these translations were so good that Bobrowski then gave the complete translation rights to the Meads, who have remained the principal translators of Bobrowski. That is an instance of how things can happen completely unexpectedly, without any publicity machine at all. Somehow the quality of the poet managed to break through all the prejudices and the ignorance, and suddenly there was a public for the book.

I'll be brief now. In the 60's there was the first book of Enzensberger's poems. First there was a pamphlet of poems in 1966, done by a small press, and then in 1968 there was a book, *Poems for People Who Don't Read Poems*, published in America and in England, and at the same time, *Selected Poems*, in that *Penguin European Poets* series. Günter Grass was also published: in 1966, *Selected Poems*; in 1969, *Poems of Günter Grass*, in the Penguin *Modern European Poets* series; and in America only, *New Poems*, 1968. I did not translate very much of Nelly Sachs' work, but did contribute to those large volumes brought out in the 60's also, when she was awarded the Nobel Prize: two volumes, *O, the Chimneys* (1967), and *The Seeker and Other Poems* (1970). My Brecht translations also began to appear in periodicals and anthologies. In book form most of them did not appear until very much later, simply because the editors of the large book of Brecht's poems published in England and America, worked on that project for about fifteen years, and so they were all delayed. I've got about sixty translations in that volume. Most of those poems had been done in the early 60's or earlier.

The poet that concerned me then for the next ten years or so is Paul Celan, whose work is so difficult to translate that I have to do it bit by bit. What happened is that I re-read all of his poems, and every time another poem became translatable, as though the poems already translated acted as keys to those so obscure to me that I was unable to translate them. And so it's taken me a long time to translate the poems that I have done by now. I also translated some prose pieces by Peter Bichsel which I found very charming, and published two of them. One is called *Really, Frau Bloom Would Very Much Like to Meet the Milkman*. The other was *There's No Such Place as America*, which was published in England as *Stories for Children*. (The German title is *Kindergeschichten*.) Unfortunately again, those books had no reception at all, as far as I know. Whether they sold or not I don't know, because in this case I don't receive royalties, but some kind of outright payment, so I don't have even those statistics to go on. What I do know is that those two books have vanished both in Britain and America, which is a great pity. Although they're much more for adults than for children, I know that my children absolutely loved those stories, and I'm sure that children would still like them now, as well as adults.

In 1973 I did an anthology of East German Poetry that included Brecht, Huchel, Kunert, Bobrowski, Kahlau, Kunze, Biermann, Volker Braun, Bartsch, Jentzsch and Sarah Kirsch. That book had, I think, a fair circulation, though it was certainly not a success as far as numbers of copies are concerned. But again there was a total lack of any kind of public reception. I scarcely remember one review of that book in America, and that I'm afraid, has been my experience in the last fifteen years or more. You cannot tell whether there are going to be any reviews at all. Whether or not a book gets reviewed, and where, seems to have become a completely arbitrary and fortuitous matter. One can no longer count on certain periodicals, as one could at one time, in Britain at any rate. I used to be able to count on the *TLS*. I knew that I could say for certain that the *TLS* would publish a review of any translation of major or merely interesting work. That is no longer the case. My recent Celan book, for example, has not been reviewed at all in the *TLS*. My Hölderlin, which reappeared in 1980, with some additional translations, was not reviewed at all. When pressure was then put by the publishers on the paper they actually produced a little note of about three lines saying that the book had appeared. And that, I'm afraid, is how it is now. If I were to talk about the reception of my work now, say over the last ten years, I should really have nothing to go on whatsoever. It would be pure guess work. So I think I'll leave it there.

Chapter Three

Workshop

Some Aspects of the Translation of Poetry

Ewald Osers
United Kingdom

I should like to make it clear from the very start that I am not a theoretician, not an *Übersetzungswissenschaftler*, but a practising translator, largely of poetry, and that such ideas as I have on the translation of poetry are derived not from theoretical concepts, either literary or translatological, but from my own working experience. However, if this illustrated talk — "lecture" seems almost too grand a description for it — were a scholarly article, then the names you would find most often in the footnotes would be those of André Lefevere, Robert de Beaugrande and James Holmes: it is their theoretical views that I share on a humbler, practical, level.

You are, of course, all familiar with Robert Frost's classical definition: "Poetry is what gets lost in translation." Obviously, neither I nor my fellow translators at this Colloquium would accept this rather defeatist quip — but since we are also readers and reviewers of translated poetry we realize that, all too often unfortunately, Robert Frost has a point.

There are, as every translator knows, innumerable ways in which a translation can go wrong. But there is no doubt in my own mind that the most common cause of translation failure in the case of poetry is connected with the transmission of the specific charge that is carried by a poetic text.

The fact that poetic language "deviates" from ordinary language was first noted by Aristotle; it was formulated, in modern linguistic

theory, by Jan Mukarovsky, who spoke of "norm and norm violation" — the norm being the whole of the linguistic system.

If — and I am deliberately over-simplifying this process — we
picture the poet intentionally violating the norm of his source
language (SL) in order to charge his text with a specific poetic
burden, then the translator, clearly, must first, in a decoding process, assess the nature and extent of this norm violation, this non-
ordinariness, and then, in a re-encoding process, endeavour to
recreate the intended effect on the target-language (TL) reader by
the choice of appropriate equivalent linguistic means.

Up to this point most theoreticians and translators would agree.
The great divide between the champions of formal correspondence
and of functional equivalence — or, as it is sometimes formulated,
an author-oriented and a reader-oriented translation — arises (or
so it seems to me) from the choice of different yardsticks. The
supporters of formal correspondence choose as their yardstick the
linguistic-poetic-cultural system of the source language, while the
supporters of functional equivalence believe that a translation must
be tested against the linguistic-poetic-cultural norm of the target-
language reader.

These two different approaches are sometimes called the Russian
theory of poetic translation and the Anglosaxon theory of poetic
translation. This, I think, is misleading. Fortunately — I mean:
fortunately for those of us who don't want to see political divisions
imposed on cultural activities — the so-called Anglosaxon theory
of poetic translation has its theoretical supporters also east of what
used to be the Iron Curtain, such as the late professor Otto Kade in
Eastern Germany, and it certainly has many practitioners in Czechoslovakia, Bulgaria and elswhere. It is, of course, true that the
Russian school of translation, notably Professor Fedorov, and in the
USA now Josef Brodsky, remain wedded to the idea of formal
equivalence at any cost, in spite of its demonstrable and demonstrated failure in certain language systems. I have myself argued
against it in Moscow, in Belgrade, in Sofia, and most recently in
Warsaw, but — in spite of massive support from James Holmes —

in vain.

This is enough theory for the moment. Let me now give you some illustrations of inadequate translations — translations which are inadequate because the "otherness," the "non-ordinariness" of the original text, and hence the emotional impact stemming from this "otherness," has not been transferred by the translator into the target-language text. Such a failure can have three different reasons: (1) the translator's failure to *recognize* the non-ordinariness of the source-language text, i.e., inadequate SL competence; (2) his inability, although he has recognized it, to reproduce it in his translation, i.e. inadequate translation competence; or (3) the absence in the TL system of analogous or otherwise appropriate linguistic structures, i.e., an objective impossibility to provide an equivalent text. The most frequent, and at the same time the most avoidable, cause is (1): the translator fails to notice, or to appreciate, the non-ordinariness of a word, or of a word in a particular context, or of a phrase.

Let me give you three examples, all of them from T.S. Eliot's *Four Quartets*.

In *East Coker* a "memory passage," a flash-back passage, ends with the lines:

> The houses are all gone under the sea,
> The dancers are all gone under the hill.

The "otherness" I am interested in here is, of course, "are gone" in both lines. The overtones of this slightly archaic construction "are gone" differ a good deal from the normal modern perfect tense "have gone." "Are gone" has something more final about it. "Have gone" still allows the thought that perhaps they may return one day; "are gone" has a permanent ring about it and, moreover, carries overtones of regret or sadness.

The German translator of the *Four Quartets*, presumably unaware of the possible alternative in the original text, unfortunately missed this aspect altogether by using "verschwanden":

Alle die Häuser verschwanden unter dem Meer.
Alle die Tänzer verschwanden unter dem Hügel.

To my ear, "verschwanden" sounds more like the result of a conjuring act than the operation of transience and time — which is
what the whole poem is about.

My next illustration is the conclusion of *East Coker*. The English
text reads:

Through the dark cold and the empty desolation,
The wave cry, the wind cry, the vast waters . . .

Here again the translator should have examined the text for non-
ordinary features. He should have noted "the dark cold" — surely
the less common way of referring to what, more often, we would
call "the cold darkness." More importantly, he should have reflected on "the wave cry, the wind cry." "Cry" is not the usual verb
associated with either waves or the wind. In ordinary speech we
expect waves to roar or to crash, and the wind to roar or to howl.
Unfortunately, the German translation misses the extra charge, the
excitement of the unaccustomed use of "cry" and has the entirely
conventional, almost cliché, rendering of "Brausen der Wellen,
Heulen des Winds."

In point of fact I would criticize the translation of this passage
on other grounds as well: (1) in addition to the lexical non-ordinariness of the use of "cry" there is also a marked element of non-ordinariness on the syntactic level: not "cry of the waves," "cry of the
wind" but "the wave cry, the wind cry" — which, again, is lost (or
missed) in "Brausen der Wellen, Heulen des Winds"; (2) the high-
pitched "cry" contrasts with the sombre sounds of "dark cold" and
"vast waters" in a way that "Brausen" and "Heulen" do not; and
(3), and perhaps most importantly, the animal or human associations of "cry", that note of anguish in "the dark cold and the empty
desolation," seem to me very important elements in the structure
of this passage.

I have no wish to "knock" Nora Wydenbruck's translation of the *Four Quartets* — there are some very fine passages in it — but a translator's failures often make better illustrations of translation problems than his or her successes.

One final illustration of the importance of spotting the "otherness" of poetic language, of the need to realize that it represents a deliberate departure from normal linguistic structures. This one is a line near the beginning of *Little Gidding*. It runs

> A glare that is blindness in the early afternoon

"A glare that is blindness" would be, in ordinary prose, "a glare that is blinding." But "blinding glare" has become a much-fingered and therefore weakened idiom, and by using the unexpected, novel, startling alternative "A glare that is blindness" Eliot restores to the image some of the original force of the word: a glare that literally blinds your eyes. To translate the line as if the common word "blinding" stood there would be quite wrong.

We have so far been arguing as if any pair of two languages always offered the same kind of alternative choices. This, of course, is not the case — as I hope to show with my next illustration. This is a Rilke poem with a strangely attention-catching opening:

> Ist ein Schloß. Das vergehende
> Wappen über dem Tor

Here, "Ist ein Schloß" is so non-ordinary that it actually strains — some might say: breaks — the rules of the German language. The first thing is to establish what prose statement the line substitutes for. Obviously it is not just a poetical shortening of "Es ist ein Schloß" — which, in German, would be the answer to the question: What is this? Nor does it stand for "Da ist ein Schloß" or "Dort ist ein Schloß." "Ist ein Schloß," with the dramatic full stop after the three words, surely means something like "Irgendwo ist ein Schloß," "Es gibt ein Schloß," "Es existiert ein Schloß."

Hence the English equivalent, the semantic equivalent, is "There is a castle." But in terms of power, of mystery if you like, of the suspense created by the three German monosyllables "Ist ein Schloß," the English information-equivalent is, of course, totally inadequate.

But what is the English translator to do with the line? The rules governing the English verb just do not permit a verb-subject sequence in a positive statement unless preceded by "There." "Is a castle" or even "Stands a castle" won't do.

I have not been able to find an English translation of this Rilke poem. (It comes from his volume *Die frühen Gedichte.*) Myself, believing discretion to be the better part of valour, would not attempt to translate it at all. But if I had to translate it, to save my life, my own strategy probably would be to operate without the verb "Ist" and to try to echo the hammer blows of "Ist ein Schloss" by a verb-less word group followed by a full stop, or indeed by the word "Castle" on its own, followed by the full stop.

> Ist ein Schloß. Das vergehende
> Wappen über dem Tor.
>
> Castle. The family's crumbling
> Heraldry over the gate.

Very inadequate, of course. An illustration of the problems which arise when certain syntactic possibilities of the source language are lacking in the target language.

This is where the theoreticians refer you to "compensatory strategies." Excellent expositions of this approach may be found in Michael Hamburger's Introduction to the Penguin edition of his Paul Celan translations, and in Robert de Beaugrande's commentary on his translation of Rilke's *Duino Elegies*. But let us admit, humbly, that there are occasions when the SL text is so SL-specific that even tolerably satisfactory patterns of equivalence are difficult or impossible to find.

I should like to mention at this point that difficulties in transferring syntactic non-ordinariness from the SL to the TL may arise not only from the non-existence of analogous structures in the TL but also from an overabundance. This does not apply to the language pair German-English, with which we are presently concerned with, but it does to some Slavic languages which — because their grammatical markers are contained in a rich system of inflexions — are exceedingly permissive as to word order. This means that a significantly non-ordinary phrase structure in the SL cannot be transmitted to the TL in this way alone, because virtually any sequence of subject-verb-object-adverbial clause would be "normal" or "expected" in the TL. This was brought home to me recently when I compared a Polish translation of Rilke's *Cornet* with the original.

We have said that, just as the communicational relevance of each part of the SL text has to be examined against the background of the SL norm, so its translation into the TL must be tested against the TL norm, against the expectation of the TL reader. This applies not only to the lexical and syntactical elements of the SL text but also to its macrostructure, such as presence or absence of metre and rhyme. Again this is not so much a problem between German and English as it is, for instance, between Russian and English, where not only the statistical frequency of rhymes differs enormously — in favour of Russian because of its inflexional character, its open syllables and its great freedom of word order — but where there is also a great difference in the contemporary reader's expectation with regard to metre-and-rhyme poetry.

Even within a given linguistic-poetic system the existence of particular rhyme pairs — as every translator of nineteenth century German lyrics knows — is entirely a matter of lexical accident. Have you ever thought what German Romantic poetry would have been like without such coincidental rhymes as "Herz"–"Schmerz," "Brust"–"Lust," "Seele"–"quäle"?

Another problem in the translation of poetry — I mean one that is specific to the translation of poetry — is polysemy, sometimes called polyvalence, the fact that very few words are true synonyms in a language pair and instead are synonymous only over an overlap area of their meanings. Take, by way of illustration, the

German word "Ruf." In its primary meaning its English equivalent is "call." Now for most non-poetic texts that fact that "Ruf" can also mean "reputation" or, in business letterheads, "telephone number" does not matter in the least — any more than the fact that "call" can also mean "visit." But in poetry words are often deliberately chosen in such a way that, on top of their primary meaning in the text, they carry the overtones, the associations, of a secondary meaning. You may think that it goes without saying that the translator, in selecting his equivalent, should bear this penumbra, this halo, of secondary meanings in mind. You would be surprised at the number of cases when this is not done.

Let me quote you an example of this polysemic trap, one that will show that a polyseme may actually have to be avoided because of a secondary meaning. Six years ago, when I reviewed Michael Hamburger's superb translations of Peter Huchel, one of only three words that I quibbled about in the whole volume was his use of "girders" for the "Pfähle", the piles, on which the buildings of Venice stand. In a letter Michael replied that "the word 'pile' had to be avoided" — clearly because of its haemorrhoidal associations. I must confess that I would probably have taken a chance with "piles." But all translation of poetry is a continuous series of decisions, of choices of the lesser evil, and hence, up to a point, subjective.

A special case of the testing of a text element for its non-ordinariness arises with metaphor. A great deal has been written about metaphor, but Aristotle's definition that it is "the name of one thing applied to another" is good enough for our purpose. Metaphor is the extension of the meaning of a word or phrase to another word or phrase. It is the principal source of the rejuvenation of language, and — to my mind at least — a measure of a language's vitality.

When we speak of "running a business," "running for the Presidency," "lending a hand," "casting an eye," "turning a blind eye" — we all use metaphor.

Like all living things, metaphor gets stale with use, loses its original impact, and becomes an ordinary idiom or even cliché.

Some linguisticians, in fact — like M. B. Dagut — want to reserve the term "metaphor" for its *first* use only, for its creative, inventive application, and argue that by the time it is lexicalized it has ceased to be a metaphor. As a practitioner I would make the point that the concepts of "metaphor" and "lexicalized idiom" are no more than abstractions, marking the starting point and the finish of a linguistic process. It is the area between these two concepts that the translator of poetry is normally concerned with, that gradual spectrum between first use and spent force, the area when a word, a group of words, or a phrase, is no longer a mint coining but not yet a fully accepted and therefore effortlessly comprehended idiom. A group of words still invested with enough of that quality of novelty, unusualness, to produce excitement, tension, an awareness that this is not just ordinary prose, though perhaps no longer producing quite the startling effect of its first use.

This, of course — since it has to do with the process of ageing — is more often a problem in diachronic translation, i.e. the translation of old text, than in the translation of contemporary poetry.

Once again it is easy enough to formulate the problem — "How new, how original, how startling, was a particular phrase when Shakespeare, or Chaucer, used it?" — and quite difficult to answer it. My own personal belief is that you can't solve the problem in any scholarly sense. Of course, there are reference books which can tell you just when the phrase "a white lie" is first attested — in other words: first used by an author whose writings have come down to us. But this doesn't tell us anything about the possible currency of the phrase in popular speech — especially as popular speech is one of the main creators of metaphor and linguistic innovation. In other words, we cannot reliably establish what *really* matters: the impact which the phrase had on contemporary readers or listeners who may, or may not, have been familiar with it.

The problem of translating across time is nearly always associated with that of translating across cultures. Let me quote a famous example: Homer's "wine-dark sea."

Anyone who has seen Retzina, the dark-red traditional Greek

wine with resin in it, will recognize the attribute. But what about translation into languages whose speakers will be puzzled by the suggestion that the sea has the colour of wine? The kind of wine *they* know? Is the translator to settle simply for "dark", or perhaps a simile of his own making, like "plum-dark"? I think not. Any really effective substitution would have to involve a liquid, or better still a beverage that is familiar to the reader but which he himself has never equated with the appearance of the sea.

But the modern translator is again only guessing. What, ideally, he would want to know is the impact of Homer's "wine-dark" on a Greek of his own time. *Was* it widely accepted that the Greek sea often had the colour of Greek wine — in the way, for instance, in which we might accept that some children have "forget-me-not-blue eyes"? Would a pre-classical Greek have gone to his local wine store to ask for an amphora of wine the colour of the sea at evening? We don't know. But my guess would be: No. "Wine-dark sea," I suspect, came to Homer's contemporaries with that startling shock of novelty and recognition that characterizes the best metaphors. It hasn't been put that way before, but it is *so* right you wonder *why* it hasn't been put that way before.

When a metaphor is brand-new, newly coined — when, therefore, it cannot yet have an equivalent in the target language — the translator, obviously, has to coin that equivalent. And, with very few exceptions, he will go for an exact, literal translation. Again, let me illustrate what I mean.

Right at the beginning of *Under Milk Wood*, Dylan Thomas describes the night in the Welsh village of Llareggub as "Bible-black" — to my mind one of countless instances of linguistic or poetic wizardry in that radio play. The English reader or listener will be familiar with the idioms "coal-black," "pitch-black," "jet-black" — but "Bible-black" at once captures his imagination. Obviously, "Bible-black" is not a new or a different colour; what the new metaphor does is illustrate the same colour, the same blackness, in a new way: the black of the familiar Bible binding. Familiar — and this is where Dylan Thomas's genius comes in — not only to his readers or listeners but much more so to the Chapel-going, sin-and-guilt-ridden people of Llareggub, the characters in his poetic radio play. By describing the night as "Bible-black" he provides a key clue to the whole atmosphere.

Erich Fried, probably the best translator of English poetry into German, has therefore, quite rightly, rendered "Bible-black" by a literal "Bibel-schwarz" — even at the cost of alliteration.

Sometimes, of course, the use of culture-linked metaphors can lead to obscurity in translation. Let me quote you two examples from my own experience. Rose Ausländer, a German poet, has a poem whose first verse, in my translation, runs as follows. Or rather: I shall stop short of the translation problem and leave the difficult words in the original:

> Weeping willows
> melancholics
> with drooping shoulders
> swaying wie Betende

In fact, we have here an illustration of more than one translation problem. Problem No. 1 is: The German substantial present participle has no gender distinction — but, since English lacks this construction except for certain verbs with a Latin root, the translator must decide whether these swaying people at prayer are masculine, feminine, or of unspecified sex.

Problem No. 2 is: What does it mean altogether? It would be interesting to discover how many among my readers understand the simile. In Rose Ausländer's native Czernowitz in the Bukowina, with — before the war — a large Jewish community, it would have been instantly understood. Jewish men sway in prayer — and, as far as I am aware, only Jewish men. Christians kneel or stand with heads bowed, muslims prostrate themselves. And Jewish women do not sway. Only the men do. That, at least, settles the first question. The translation must be "like men at prayer" and not, for instance, "like people at prayer."

But should the translator go further, in terms of interpretation?

Should one say "like Jews at prayer," or "like men in a synagogue," or something of that kind?

"Swaying like men at prayer" would, I think, be meaningful to educated readers — and, of course, also to non-Jews since we all know a little about each other's cultural and religious traditions — in London, Manchester, New York and Melbourne. But what about Delhi, in the numerically largest country with English still one of the official languages? Indians are motionless in prayer. Or what about the American Bible belt?

But if one takes another look at the German original one realizes that it faces the same problem within its own linguistic sphere. The number of Jews — and certainly Jews given to orthodox observance and customs — in post-war Germany and Austria is so small that the phrase, even among Rose Ausländer's German readership, must hover on the edge between comprehension and bemused guessing. I may as well admit that I decided, quite simply, on

Swaying like men at prayer

Another illustration, also from my own experience. A few years ago, when I translated a volume of 13th century Armenian love poetry I repeatedly encountered the phrase: "Your breasts are a cathedral." Now to the English, or American, reader the word cathedral conjures up the Gothic spires of Salisbury, or Ulm, or Cologne, or else the massive square towers of Notre Dame de Paris, or Chartres, or Lincoln, or Durham — neither of them a shape that any girl I know would like her breasts to be. But, of course, the medieval cathedrals of Armenia had cupped domes — not the huge hemispheric cupolas of St. Peter's or of Muslim mosques, but the flattened domes also found on some Byzantine churches — which made this metaphor entirely natural and totally unforced to the Armenian poet and to his audience. Oversimplifying a little, I had basically three choices: (1) stick to the text and bewilder, or at best bemuse, the reader; (2) add an explanatory footnote — something I hate doing because I feel it ruins the immediacy of poetic impact; or (3) — and this is what I did — amplify the translation to "the domes of a cathedral."

I should like to add that this kind of explication is — in my Credo — permissible only when it serves to impart, or restore, to the translation the same degree of accessibility as that enjoyed by the original. It should not, I believe, be practised to facilitate the comprehensibility of the translation above that of the original. Any "undefinedness" or mysteriousness or opacity inherent in the original poem, whether deliberate or growing organically out of the poet's handling of his linguistic material, should of course be carried across into the translation. This assessment of "reader accessibility" must be one of the most difficult judgements to perform — I say: "must be" because I don't often encounter it in the poetry that appeals to me, whereas Michael Hamburger must have faced this problem continuously, both with Hölderlin and with Celan.

I should like to conclude with another example of a cross-cultural problem. Like my first few illustrations this, too, comes from T.S. Eliot.

A poem written by Eliot in 1920, and entitled *A Cooking Egg*, ends with the lines

> Over buttered scones and crumpets
> Weeping, weeping multitudes
> Droop in a hundred A.B.C.'s

Eliot, an American by birth, had by then become very much an Englishman. On a lecture tour in the spring of 1977 I tried these three lines on audiences at 10 United States universities, to discover if they could make any sense of them. Roughly half the audience in each place knew what "scones" were; between one-third and a half knew what "crumpets" were. But no one, with the exception of two English people, understood the reference to the A.B.C.'s. Yet to Eliot's English readers an "A.B.C." was as instantly comprehensible as a "Howard Johnson" would be to an American or Canadian. It was a chain of restaurants, or tea rooms, inexpensive but with an air of refinement; one sat at little tables, not at the bar.

If these English lines are obscure even to readers using another version of the English language — and, I suspect, are becoming increasingly obscure even to a younger generation of English readers who have grown up since the disappearance of the A.B.C.s — what is the translator into another language to do with them? How should he render this specifically English institution — specifically English, that is, for afternoon tea with buttered scones and crumpets? Let us see what the German translator has done. In German the lines read:

> Weinend, weinend in hellen Scharen
> Sitzt das gebeugt vor Huhn, Pommefrits und Pils —
> Die Menschmillionen in ein hundert Hühnergrills.

Literally translated: Weeping, weeping multitudes / sitting bent over chicken, french fried, and lager / in a hundred chicken grills. The translator, Eva Hesse, is usually a good translator but here, I think, she has gone totally wrong. By turning the tea place into a chicken grill she misses — in my view — Eliot's point.

Buttered scones and crumpets in an A.B.C. are very different from a meal in a chicken grill: they are, or were in Eliot's day, something between meals, an almost ritualized pause between finishing one's working day and commuting home. The "weeping, weeping multitudes" are the office workers and shop workers who have just put another day behind them and who, during their unwinding ritual of tea and crumpets, are suddenly overcome by the dreariness, the drabness, the frustration and the emptiness of their lives. Eliot's vision, to my mind, is very different from the purposeful eaters in a Kentucky Fried Chicken place. So different that one wonders what the German reader can make of all those tears shed over chicken, french fried and lager.

I do not want to be misunderstood. Eliot's "A.B.C.'s" obviously had to be represented by some other institution, one familiar to the reader. My complaint is not that the translator has transposed the scene into a different setting but that she has transposed it into a wrong setting, one with the wrong atmosphere and associations. The keynote of Eliot's passage is not the food intake but the brief stop, the moment of "neutral" between "office gear" and "domestic gear," the vulnerable in-between moment. There may be no exact cultural equivalent — indeed the whole custom of "unwinding" may be peculiar to "commuting societies" — but I should have thought that the cocktail lounge in the U.S.A., the pavement café in France, and the *Kaffeehaus* or *Konditorei* in Germany and Austria would be much closer equivalents in terms of atmosphere and psychological function.

You will have gathered from what I have said that I believe that the nature of translation problems can be pinpointed, analysed and studied, and that strategies for tackling them — or, at least, the generic ones — can be mapped out. But I do not believe that anything like a detailed tactic, blueprint or drill — one that would be applicable to all situations — can ever be developed. Within a broad general strategy specific solutions must always remain intuitive.

Translating Hildesheimer's *Mozart*

Marion Faber
Swarthmore, Pennsylvania

This paper has a two-fold purpose: first, I would like to present a method of translation, and analyse a procedure which I have found effective in translating. Second, I would like to address some particular problems of the specific translation which led to these observations, namely my translation of Wolfgang Hildesheimer's 1977 biography *Mozart*.[1] The two parts of my paper are not particularly inter-related, but that may also be in the nature of the beast: attempts to define the act of translation, to develop theories of the elusive process we engage in when we do it, generally cannot comprehend the voluminous and disparate examples of those problems and choices which go into each translation. For when all is said and done, that is what translation is *in practice*: a continual act of compromise, a continual search, rejection, renewed search, reluctant acceptance (or sometimes delighted acceptance) of particular *decisions*, particular *solutions*. To include all these infinite decisions within certain all-encompassing categories, must prove impossible.[2]

As I mentioned, the procedure followed was for the translation of Wolfgang Hildesheimer's biography *Mozart*. True, this is not literature in the strict sense of a work falling within the tree genres of prose fiction, poetry, or drama. But the work is as much an essay as a biography in the narrow sense, and the essay is indeed a genre more and more gaining recognition for the artistic challenge and spe it represents. (One thinks of Hofmannsthal or Thomas Mann.) In this sense, then, it deserves to be included within the realm of literature. And Hildesheimer's essayistic meditation on the life and phenomenon of Mozart can surely be considered literature, written, as it is, by an established playwright, novelist, and short story writer, and presenting many of the same aesthetic problems as a more conventionally literary work. But first, the outline of a method.

In his work *Einbahnstraße*, Walter Benjamin makes the following observation, under the sub-title, "Achtung Stufen!":

> Arbeit an einer guten Prosa hat drei Stufen: eine musikalische, auf der sie komponiert, eine architektonische, auf der sie gebaut, endlich eine textile, auf der sie gewoben wird.[3]

Clearly, the three stages described here refer to a good prose of one's *own* composing. And in "Die Aufgabe des Übersetzers,"[4] Benjamin distinguished very clearly between the act of writing and the act of translating. Their relationship to language is quite different. Nevertheless I would like to apply Benjamin's conception of the writer's task to that of the translator as well, for I believe the analogy is as fitting, and beyond that, may even be useful in sketching out a method for translation in general.

The first stage, Benjamin writes, is the musical stage. For the writer, this must represent an abstract conception, the overall shape, the idea, the direction that his thought will take. For the translator, no differently, the first stage of translating must be musical, in that the abstract totality, the line, the direction is the primary concern in rendering the thought of another in one's own language. Thus, the first stage in translation must be swift, almost pre-conscious to some degree, and, to lapse briefly into the utterly quotidian, written out by hand. It should be written as quickly as possible, with almost no time to stop or reflect or consider. As implied in the analogy with music, the first stage is concerned with sound and rhythm, with an *intuitive* matching of emphasis, weight, balance, pace. Like music, the text should flow at this stage, whatever the cost, reproducing cadences, fluency, and, above all, the "voice" used in the original. In the case of Hildesheimer, this means an ironic, witty, at times painfully self-conscious and reflective, involuted voice. That tone, the capturing of it, is the first concern — again reaffirming the musical analogy. Because this *tone* is the most intuitive aspect of understanding, within one's own language or inter-lingually, and because one's first, immediate response is often the most accurate, being the most intuitive, this first stage, I believe, is essential, even if further stages ultimately determine that the greater part of what appears in this first form is in need of re-casting.

The second stage is called by Benjamin the architectonic, and refers, I would presume, to the writer's restructuring his concepts, building thought upon thought, with considered transitions, arguments, or other elements, essential to give the initially musical substance firmness, stability, weight. In the act of translation, this second stage is on the one hand the building up of the accuracy of the translation. Once the contours are established, the task is now to consult aids (dictionaries, thesauruses, lexicons) for exact nuances of words, for words used idiosyncratically or not in common usage, or whose exact English meaning is unsure. The second task in this stage is to re-structure phrases and sentences so that the translation reads like more or less comprehensible English (which may not always be the case in the first stage), with each element of the sentence at least prosaically correct. In other words, the focus here, as in Benjamin's analogy, is more on the individual parts of the text, the "bricks" which go to make up the structure, rather than on the overall shape.

At this point, renewed distance from the text in question is necessary, distance which a clean typed copy can provide. With this before the translator, like a piece of cloth, the third, or textile step of the procedure can be undertaken. Here, as in the last stage of crocheting an afghan or weaving a wall hanging, the threads are tucked in, the texture made smooth (or suitably rough, if that is what the design demands); the details are addressed and put in order. This revision aims at emphasis, power, clarity, in the English.

By this time, too, the meaning — in English — of the text has become more inherent, better assimilated in the translator, and he can afford a pleasurable attention to minutiae, the questions of good English style. As Benjamin suggests, this third stage provides the pleasure of certain kinds of needlework. Painstaking stitches, rather than bricks or melodies, are now the medium of endeavor.

To sum it up, Stage One addresses the spirit of the original text; Stage Two the accuracy of the translation; Stage Three its style. These three steps are of course not distinct — aspects of each make up the others. And all three stages are, I believe, as relevant to the translator's task as to the writer's.

When these steps in Benjamin's brief aperçu have been taken, the translation still has a long way to go. Three further stages of editing and revision are imperative.

First, an English-language reader, preferably with no knowledge of German, should edit the text. The translator is deluded all too easily into thinking that sentences which satisfy him are also lucid to the English-language reader in general. For there is no way that the translator can keep the original German out of his head; he will be tempted to retain words, phrases, or whole clauses for the sake of some memory of their correspondence to the original, elements which to the objective reader make no sense, are clumsy and awkward, or oblique and obscure.

Take this passage from the German, for example:

> Mozart als einmaliges Phänomen — von diesem Gemeinplatz kommen wir nicht los. Er sei hier nicht als Ausdruck der Schwärmerei angewandt, sondern im Versuch, einen Standort der Klassifikation zu finden, wobei die Vergeblichkeit des Versuches das Resultat vorwegnimmt.

The translator might come up with something like this version:

> We cannot get free of the cliché of Mozart as a totally unique phenomenon. May it be understood here not as the phrase of an enthusiast, but as the attempt to find a firm classification, the futility of any attempt preparing us for the result.

If brought to one's attention, it will soon become clear that this is an impossible English sentence. Usually, the next step involves a more violent handling of the original, an attempt to get behind the *words* and seize the meaning and then wrestle that meaning into comprehensible English.

Thus the example mentioned may be improved as follows:

> We cannot get free of the cliché of Mozart as a totally unique phenomenon. We use it here not as enthusiastic gushing, but in order to show the futility of any narrow attempt at classification.

This version, too, may stand some re-working, but there is the sense, at least, that this effort is nearer the goal.

The second of the three further stages includes an appeal to experts with knowledge beyond translator's, in this particular case, to a musicologist, a psychologist, and a native German. It is not always possible to have recourse to the "Stifter" himself, the author of the original text, but in this case, Hildesheimer was a gracious source of reference. He is quite fluent in English, though unfamiliar with American usage (e.g., the use of the past participle "gotten"). I will refer to some of his answers to questions about various points shortly.

The last of these three final stages is the contribution of the publisher-editor. Although it may well not be the case with translators of greater experience, in my own case I found the editor's excising hand to be quicker and bolder than my own. The translator, it seemed to me, owes first allegiance to the text, to render it faithfully as it appeared in print. The editor, I learned, seems to feel this first allegiance in a different way; that is, to the text as it will be read by a new audience. He cut, for example, not only mundane superfluities in Hildesheimer's style, discursiveness that wandered, however slightly, from the point, but also whole sentences which he felt would embarrass the author in the eyes of the American reading public. Franz Rosenzweig[5] once observed that the translator is the servant of two masters: the original text and his audience; hence the agony of his position. The editor, however, seems to be less divided, and can deal more severely with his "product."

At times this can rob the original of its unique — if not exotic — quality. For example, Hildesheimer speaks of Mozart as a "Genie eines geheimen Sich-Versagens," by which he means (as he made clear in a letter) a "genius of a secret self-concealment." The editor apparently found this too foreign a formulation in English, and changed the phrase to a "genius at self-concealment." True, it might read better, but the German implication that self-concealment is part of Mozart's *nature,* a quality residing in him, which is captured by the use of the genitive, is now externalized, and even diffused a bit by the editor's concern for fluency in the English.

To address now some other problems in the translation of this work: one pervasive problem is that its author, being a creative writer of imagination, seeks to incorporate musical terminology, even musical forms into this biography of the musician Mozart. Thus he continually refers to the "score of Mozart's life," the "range" ("Skala" or sometimes "Register") of his emotions, the "Engführung" of an argument, etc. In general, these references, "Anspielungen," are more difficult to render gracefully in English, and sometimes they result in obliqueness and even ambiguity in the German. For example, on page 66 Hildesheimer writes about a phrase in Mozart's letter to a friend describing the death of his mother:

> Über den Tod seiner Mutter schrieb er an Bullinger . . . : "Gott hat es
> so haben wollen", aber es klingt halbherzig, wie immer, wenn er
> über Gottes Willen spricht. Was er meint, ist: "Es hat eben so sein
> sollen"; eine Floskel, die zwar nichts sagt, die aber die Quelle seiner
> Reaktionen genauer wiedergibt als alle anderen Motive.

When setting down to render this in English, one asks initially: 'What is meant by "Motive"?' Motives, in the sense of reasons, motivations; or motives in the sense of musical themes, phrases? Hildesheimer was able to clear up the dilemma:

> Motiv war hier quasi-musikalisch gemeint, aber nun finde ich es
> auch ungenau. Genauer wäre "Angaben seiner Motive" [Here it is

clearly no longer meant musically], aber auch das ist nicht gut. "An-
gaben seiner Gefühle" wäre wohl das Richtige. Mit Angabe meine
ich die Fassung in Worte, die Formulierung. "Formulierungen
seiner Empfindungen" wäre wohl das beste — deutsch klingt es
natürlich nicht schön.

In this case, then, the act of intuiting, which always plays so large
a role in the act of translation, had to comprehend as well the act
of *musical* intuiting, the correlation of a frame of musical analogies
to Hildesheimer's insights (dense in their own right) about this
historical figure.

A second example of such musical imagery concerns the word
"obligat." On p. 188 Hildesheimer uses it in its musical sense ("eine
obligate Klarinetten- oder Bassetthornstimme"), while on the very
next page there is a reference to the "obligates Männergesangs-
vereinspensum für die Freimaurer." A clear head might easily
distinguish the two different senses of the word in these cases, but
given a head which had already grappled with 187 pages of such
ambiguous semantic uses of musical and psychological homo-
nyms, it is perhaps understandable if the translator begins to doubt
what *ought* to be clear.

In addition to musical metaphors, there were plays on words in
German, which it was always a challenge to reproduce. In some
cases, alliteration: "Strümpfe stopfen und Wäsche waschen" becomes "patch his pockets and launder his linen," for example.
Many such poetic touches had to be sacrificed, however. In a work
more strictly literary that might not be the case; for then the content
could be said to depend on them more heavily. Here, they seemed
less important to the whole than the lucid rendering of the content
as divorced from its form.

As with so many texts, this one too posed problems concerning
references familiar in the original language, with no relevance for
the English-language reader. Two solutions were appropriate.
When Hildesheimer writes that Mozart told his superiors to their
face what he really thought of them, he remarks, "Zivilcourage ist
einer ihrer (legend's) liebsten Gegenstände, seit dem Müller von

Sanssouci." There will not be many English-language readers who
will pick up the reference to the anecdote about the plucky Miller
and Frederick the Great, and to re-tell it would take too long — so
it is probably best omitted. When, on the other hand, Hildesheimer
writes on p. 64 that "Ihm (Mozart) gab kein Gott zu sagen, was er
leide," this reference to Goethe's *Tasso*, described as such, is easily
incorporated into the translation.

The translator's other perennial problem, what to do with incon-
sistencies, inaccuracies, errors in the original, was also a concern
here. "Goneril" should have been "Cordelia," "Don Basilio," "Don
Curzio." One last example of the assistance the author provided:
In his discussion of the *Zauberflöte*, Hildesheimer writes:

> Das Singspiel ist niemals ein formal glückliches Gebilde gewesen.
> Der Sprechtext, der die Handlung zu fördern hat, fordert auch den
> Zerfall des musikalischen Kontinuums: Nummer bleibt Nummer.
> Und in der *Zauberflöte* kann ihre thematische Vielfalt dem diffusen
> Anspruch nicht gerecht werden.

In response to my question: To what does "*ihre* thematische Vielfalt" refer, he writes:

> "Ihre" bezieht sich auf die Handlung, zwei Zeilen zuvor, also auf
> die Verschiedenheit der Nummern. Anspruch ist hier, soweit ich es
> beurteilen kann, sowohl "claim" als auch "pretension," denn man
> kann "Anspruch" sowohl als den Anspruch deuten, den wir an das
> Werk stellen, als auch den, mit dem das Werk auftritt, jedenfalls ist
> er diffus [indistinct? vague?]. Wir können ihn nicht festlegen. Die
> "thematische Vielfalt," d.h. die wechselnde Distanz, die jede Num-
> mer verlangt - und zwar wohl von *uns* als auch von dem *Komponis-*
> *ten* - bedeutet eine dauernde Umstellung in *unserer Rezeption* und im
> Vertonungsanspruch des *Komponisten,* einen dauernden Wechsel in
> *unserer* und in *seiner* Verteilung der Sympathie und Antipathie.

Given this information, the final English version reads:

> The Singspiel never was a satisfactory formal structure. The spoken
> text, which must further the action, also furthers the collapse of the
> musical continuity. A number can be no more than a number. And
> the diversity of action in *Die Zauberflöte* cannot render the opera's
> vague claims more consistent.

This particular problem moved Hildesheimer to comment:

I really begin to wonder what the Japanese or the Finnish translator has done about – say – the "diffusen Anspruch." What will they do about the *letters?!* How does "Dreck, oh Dreck, oh süßes Wort . . ." sound in Japanese?!

A word in conclusion. Ingmar Bergman, when asked which of his films he had most enjoyed making, answered "The Magic Flute." It was wonderful, he said, to be able to have Mozart in the editing room every day. Translating *Mozart*, for all the agony of the effort to do justice to its weighty and often brilliant arguments, without being crushed by their abstractness, expressed in processions of nouns, likewise provided a double pleasure: the subject was Mozart, the author Wolfgang Hildesheimer.

NOTES

1. Wolfgang Hildesheimer, *Mozart* (Frankfurt: Suhrkamp, 1977), 416 pages. My English-language translation has been published by Farrar, Straus and Girous, New York, 1982. All quotations from *Mozart* refer to these two editions.

2. The method of working I describe, based on my personal experience, has marked similarities to what Eugene A. Nida describes in his work *Towards a Science of Translation* (Leiden: Brill, 1964). See especially pp. 246f.

3. Walter Benjamin, *Einbahnstraße* (Frankfurt: Suhrkamp, 1955), pp. 39f.

4. Walter Benjamin, "Die Aufgabe des Übersetzers", in *Gesammelte Schriften*, IV, 1 (Frankfurt: Suhrkamp, 1972), pp. 9-21.

5. Franz Rosenzweig, in *Translating Literature: The German Tradition*, ed. by A. Lefevere (Assen: Van Gorcum, 1977), p. 110.

Satire in Translation

Kurt Tucholsky and Karl Kraus

Harry Zohn
Brandeis University, Massachusetts

Twenty-five years ago, when I was looking for a publisher for my translations from the prose of the Berlin-born satirist Kurt Tucholsky and was dispiritedly accumulating rejection slips, the editor of one publishing house wrote me that he personally loved to read satire but in his professional capacity shied away from it. Presumably, so I reflected sardonically, such high-risk material would have to be assigned to a publisher by law for that gentleman to continue to indulge his tastes. If George S. Kaufman's celebrated dictum "Satire is what closes Saturday night" has any validity, a similar subsidy would have to be provided for the theater. There has been much in my experience during the past two or three decades to convince me that while Juvenal's words *Difficile est saturam non scribere* have rung down the centuries, a would-be writer of satire had better resist the impulse, or else write for his own satisfaction only. If it is hard not to write satire, it appears to be even harder to publish, teach, or translate it. It evidently is "caviar to the general," and even when it is published, it seems fated to be rejected, rebated, and remaindered more often than it is reviewed or reissued.

This seeming paradox at a time that "cries out for satire," to use a Tucholskyan phrase, may be explainable in part by the rather general confusion as to what satire is and what it can or cannot do. C.E. Vulliamy believes that "ages of peril and disillusionment such as our own are less productive of genuine satire, though equally productive of mere vituperation; and literary satire is almost extinct, or so anemic as to be scarcely viable."[1] On the other hand, Edgar Johnson writes: "in periods of widespread change, things are subjected to a critical overhauling. Altering social institutions and conventional beliefs leads to criticism, and criticism begets satire. . . . The satiric note is a characteristic strain in the babel of the modern world"[2] The disagreement expressed here is probably more apparent than real: Vulliamy is referring to satire as a literary form, Johnson to satire as the temper of the times. But there can be little doubt that satirists have fallen on evil times — and not only the virtually non-existent satirists of our own day, who really cannot exist in view of the fact that the bedrock of sanity which must serve as the launching pad for their satirical barbs has turned into quicksand. Tucholsky's question and answer "What may satire do? Anything" ("Was darf die Satire? Alles") is not being taken seriously, and contemporary critics and historians like Walter Laqueur and Gordon Craig blame Tucholsky for having been the *enfant terrible* of the Weimar Republic who helped bring it down by stunting its fragile growth with his satirical sallies. Another American critic, Ernst Pawel, comes to the preposterous conclusion — preposterous in the face of so much European evidence to the contrary — that Kurt Tucholsky's work is "the record of a dead world in a dead language, increasingly difficult to decipher."[3] (The above-mentioned American editor, incidentally, also opined that since Americans were so secure, self-sufficient, and optimistic, they would not have much use for a Tucholsky; one wonders whether he still feels this way after Vietnam, Watergate, and Teheran.)

The Viennese satirist Karl Kraus, in turn, has been attached for his intemperance, his "Jewish self-hatred," for turning mole-hills into mountains and bringing up heavy artillery to take potshots at sparrows. Both Tucholsky and Kraus were essentially apolitical men. The Berliner abandoned his native city and country as early as the mid-twenties and took his own life in exile ten years later; the man who, like Sigmund Freud, had a love-hate relationship to Vienna was, in his final years, expected to stop Hitlerism with a special isuue of *Die Fackel*, the periodical he edited for over three decades (and wrote himself for two and a half). Curiously enough, the erstwhile sympathizer with Social Democracy in his last years found himself in the corner of Austro-Fascism, presumably the lesser of two evils. The two satirists died within six months of each other — in 1935 and 1936 respectively. They were dissimilar in many ways and did not admire each other despite their contemporaneousness and certain common causes (both were, after all, moral agents and social scavengers "working on a storage of bile," to use Meredith's phrase.) What they really shared — in addition to the German language, which they used so virtuosically — was silence during their last years. Both Tucholsky and Kraus fell silent and all but stopped writing after 1933, when it became increasingly plain that the *Zeitgeist* was not only incommensurable with *Geist* as they conceived of it but was indeed making war on the human spirit. "The word expired when that world awoke" — this is how Kraus put it in his last poem.[4]

Max Eastman's pithy definition of satire, "Humor as a weapon,"[5] is applicable to both writers. Certainly Tucholsky regarded language as a weapon, and so did Kraus, though his weapon was the exposure of threats to language as well as the defense of language. The particular challange to the translator derives from the fact that he is dealing with highly charged material; he must actually fashion a carefully crafted weapon in another language, one made of other material, and must see to it that it is not blunted in transit and has comparable sharpness. This presupposes sympathy with the satiric stance. More than with other types of literature, the translator of satire needs to be in tune or in accord with the satirist. If you are doing to serve "freche Hunde," your bite must be at least a match for your bark. Head-shaking nice Nellies, male and female, cannot be effective translators of satire, nor can "auf der Ka-lauer liegende Einfallspinsel" (if I may presume to collaborate with Karl

Kraus on some verbal play). Kraus, the man who hauled so many of his contemporaries, the powerful and the pitiful alike, before a tribunal of total satire, has for too long been deemed essentially untranslatable, for in his case it is not just a question of language as a weapon, but of the Word, the German language itself, as the bearer of an entire ethical system that largely defies effective transplantation. Erich Heller has explained this quite eloquently: "Karl Kraus did not write 'in a language,' but through his the beauty, profundity, and accumulated moral experience of the German language assumed personal shape and became the crucial witness in the case this inspired prosecutor brought against his time."[6]

Surely this kind of challenge ought to inspire translators to try for what John Ciardi has termed "the best possible failure," and I am among the very few who have made such attempt. Surely any translator must despair of doing justice to a writer who has said: "The closer the look one takes at a word, the greater the distance from which it looks back."[7] Yet in recent years enough translators with the necessary competence, venturesomeness, and satiric instinct have appeared to make even men like Erich Heller and George Steiner modify their conviction of Kraus's untranslatability. A volume of Karl Kraus in English appeared as early as 1930 (*Poems*, translated by Albert Bloch); by now there are five such volumes devoted to Kraus and four to Tucholsky, each containing selections carefully culled from their enormous *oeuvres* to ensure only minimal losses in the linguistic transplantation and to minimize the necessity for extended explanatory notes.

But have Kurt Tucholsky and Karl Kraus been given their due within the canon of world satire available to readers of English? They have not; they are, in fact, all but non-existent as far as studies or anthologies produced in this country are concerned, not to mention the availability (or non-availability) in North American bookstores of what little of their work has appeared inEnglish. With but a few exceptions one gets the impression that English-language satire is the only kind that matters. Leonard Feinberg, author of *The Satirist: His Temperament, Motivation and Influence* (Iowa State University Press, 1964) seems never to have heard of the Berliner and the Viennese. The same is true of the well-read and urbane Gilbert Highet, whose *Anatomy of Satire* (Princeton University Press, 1962) bespeaks an acquaintance with such fairly arcane Germanic figures as Abraham a Sancta Clara, Grimmelshausen, Lichtenberg, and the Captain of Köpenick but not with the two foremost German-language satirists since Heinrich Heine. One would, of course, expect the classicist Highet to give pride of place to the Greco-Roman tradition, and this tradition is not neglected in such comprehensive collections as Edgar Johnson's *Satire* and Vulliamy's *The Anatomy of Satire*, where there are also the customary bows to other translated authors, such as Cervantes, Voltaire, and Anatole France. But who are Johnson's prime exemplars of twentieth-century satire? Max Beerbohm, Sinclair Lewis, Ring Lardner, Dorothy Parker, Thomas Wolfe, and James Thurber. *Satire, that Blasted Art,* edited by John R. Clark and Anna Motto (New York, 1973), draws its examples from world literature and devotes a few pages to Heine and Kafka, but Arthur Pollard's little volume on satire in the series *The Critical Idiom* (London 1970) leads one to believe that satire has been written only in English. *Satire: A Critical Anthology,* edited by John Russell and Ashley Brown (Cleveland, 1967), contains Heine and Kafka (about whom we are told that "he went to the front in World War I and virtually destroyed his health")[8] but not Tucholsky or Kraus.

There is, *mirabile dictu,* one book in which both Kraus and Tucholsky rate brief mention: Matthew Hodgart's wide-ranging and nicely illustrated book on satire in the World University Library (London, 1969). But even this presentation is flawed. For one thing, Tucholsky is mentioned only as a poet; as such, sad to say, he has not benefitted from the recent American revival of interest in the literary and political cabaret of yesteryear and is at best a name to those who have become quite familiar with Bert Brecht, Kurt Weill, and George Grosz. (A few years ago he did "close Saturday night" off-off-Broadway. A revue based on Tucholsky's marvelous chansons with the cutesy title "Tickles by Tucholsky" was scuttled there

by a Germanophobe, i.e., a hostile Israeli director, an uncomprehen-
ding and incompetent "name" actress, a misguided musical director who arranged the settings of Hanns Eisler, Olaf Bienert, and
others in the style of an oompapah band, and an indifferent, know-
nothing press.) For another thing, one of the two Kraus aphorisms
quoted by Hodgart (who calls it "one of the best jokes about the
Freudians") is blunted by mistranslation: "Psychoanalysis is that
disease of which it pretends to be the cure."[9] It should, of course,
read "mental illness" and not just "disease." Other versions translate *Geisteskrankheit* as "spiritual disease." But such versions still
are far preferable to the crippling mistranslation which has by now
disgraced umpteen printings of Rollo May's book *Love and Will*:
"Psychoanalysis is in fact that illness of which its therapy purports
to be the cure" — or to the "free translation" offered by Thomas
Szasz in his curiously distorted and misleading book on Kraus:
"Before Freud, doctors cautioned that the cure may be worse than
the disease; now they ought to caution that there is a cure which is
a disease — namely psychoanalysis."[10] What happens to a pithy,
hard-hitting satiric statement when such extended, verbose, edi-
torializing, "elucidative," self-serving treatment is inflicted upon
it?[11] Hodgart, incidentally, believes that there have been only few
satirists in German-speaking countries. Yet Helmut Arntzen has
included in *Gegen-Zeitung*, his monumental anthology of German
satire of the twentieth century (Heidelberg, 1964), 66 satiric writers,
31 of whom were driven out of their native country; and since 23
of the 66 were already dead or not yet active in 1933, fully two-
thirds of these satirists were rejected — or worse — by their country. Surely this fact is quite revealing and instructive. It is not
surprising that the work of Kraus and Tucholsky, so widely dis-
seminated in Europe today, should loom large in Arntzen's anthology, for from their satire one can learn a great deal about the dying
decades of the Austro-Hungarian empire, the troubled first Austrian republic, and the no less troubled Weimar Republic. But the
enduring value of their satire really derives from its mordant depic-
tion of human nature with an altogether humanistic and huma-

nitarian intent. It comes as a pleasant surprise that in a recent novel Aharon Appelfeld, a European-born Israeli writer, sensed just this in the work of one of these two "lapsed Jews" when he writes: "If anyone deserved the title of a great . . . it was Karl Kraus; he had revived satire . . . the only art form appropriate to our lives."[12]

The fact remains that it is impossible to convey the full force of satirists whose work is to such a large extent tied to their own language; yet enough can be Englished to bring out the universal relevance of their satire and perhaps even some of their craftsmanship. One hopes that Kraus's aphorism about a linguistic work rendered into another language being comparable to someone crossing a border without one's skin and putting on the local garb on the other side is a half-truth rather than one-and-a-half truths (an aphorism, according to Kraus, being either one or the other).

A few examples may serve to clarify both Kraus's imaginative response to language and the difficulties inherent in transferring this response to another language. I rendered the aphorism "Man lebt nicht einmal einmal" as "You don't live even once"; the trite German saying "Man lebt nur einmal," which has an English equivalent in the (equally trite) hedonistic saying "You live only once" (heard more frequently as "You only live once") has been turned around by Kraus. The English translation seems to reflect a pessimistic *Weltanschauung*, the kind of mere opinion that Kraus abhorred. Yet the satirist has utilized the possibilities of the German language to give verbal play to an idea derived directly from this language: *einmal*, stressed on the first syllable and meaning "once," is receded by the same word, stressed on the second syllable and meaning — in conjunction with the negation *nicht* — "not even." To reproduce the syntactical uniqueness of German and still convey Kraus's thought (which is basically life-affirming in a sad, rueful way), one would have to use the analogous (though admittedly not fully equivalent) resources of the English language, ending up with a version of Kraus's aphorism that would read something like this: "Your chances of living a full, happy, productive life are not even even." But would this still be a *translation*? Another case in point where an English rendition at best results in a compromise which, however ingenious, cannot do full justice to a devastatingly witty idea is Kraus's aphorism "Je größer der Stiefel, desto größer der Absatz." On the face of it, this is a shoemaker's truism: "The bigger the boot, the bigger the heel." But in colloquial German, *Stiefel* also means "blather" or "balderdash," and another meaning of *Absatz* is "sale." My translation, "The bigger the bull, the bigger the bull market," still does not convey all the levels of meaning and the language-derived ideas in Kraus's aphorism, especially when one considers that another meaning of *Absatz* is "paragraph." (In view of Kraus's interminable paragraphs, the satirist's detractors might well use this aphorism against him!)

If I may indulge in a bit of workshop talk not directly related to Kraus or Tucholsky, I should like to point out that sympathy and experience with satire will often lead a translator to identify and reproduce satiric elements in texts that may not in themselves be satires. If a translator is fortunate enough to work with a living writer, he may secure that writer's approval and perhaps even collaboration in the service of satire. Some twenty years ago I had that experience with the contemporary Austrian writer and psychologist Walter Toman. One of Toman's stories deals with undertakers who resort to dubious advertising practices and even invent a "motorized corpse" in an effort to increase their business. This translator's contribution started with the title of that story, "Esprit de Corpse"[13] and proceeded to advertising slogans like "We lay you out with the least outlay," "A-tisket, a-tasket, who's got the nicest casket?" and "DeHaven makes it the perfect exit." In "Juli-Sonntag im Prater," a bleak picture of Vienna's celebrated pleasure ground, Theodor Herzl does a bit of amateur psychologizing and describes a rather joyless lower-class family. He speculates that the man may be a butcher who married a girl with all the attractiveness of a boss's daughter: "Er schnitt es gern in jeden Schinken ein." This is an easily recognizable reference to a line from "Ungeduld," a song from the Schubert-Müller song cycle *Die schöne Müllerin* ("Ich schnitt es gern in alle Rinden ein.") To reproduce Herzl's somewhat sardonic pun, an equivalent phrase from the literature or popular culture of English-speaking countries must be found, and this phrase must contain a reference to some article familiar to an unlettered butcher which he might use to express his love. After a great deal of reflection, I came up with two possible translations, adaptations of two song titles: "To him, love was a many-rendered thing" and "Two hearts beat in three-quarter rind." Since Herzl wrote his piece in the 1890s and both songs are of much more recent vintage, each translation involves an anachronism, but the reference to the Robert Stolz song at least preserves the Viennese ambiance.

Verbal play is, of course, always a challenge, but it is one that can often be met successfully and memorably. Consider, for example, this epigrammatic poem by Erich Kästner:

> Das ist das Verhängnis:
> Zwischen Empfängnis
> Und Leichenbegängis
> Nichts als Bedrängnis.

Here is Patrick Bridgewater's rendition:

> This is destination:
> Between procreation
> And inhumation
> Nothing but vexation.

And here is mine:

> The curse of creation:
> 'Twixt procreation
> And cremation
> Just aggravation.[14]

On the face of it, the last sentence of Kurt Tucholsky's "Märchen" (his first published work, 1907) conveys the idea that the emperor in question quite literally "gave a hoot" on a flute. But the satiric idea that the young Tucholsky wished to convey about Wilhelm II is that the rather philistine emperor put such an unusual articitc and aesthetic item to mundane use. The point is that he didn't give a hoot about it, and so my translation had to change the flute into another object:

Märchen

Es war einmal ein Kaiser, der über ein unermeßich großes, reiches und schönes Land herrschte. Und er basaß wie jeder andere Kaiser auch eine Schatzkammer, in der inmitten all der glänzenden und glitzernden Juwelen auch eine Flöte lag. Das war aber ein merkwürdiges Instrument. Wenn man nämlich durch eins der vier Löcher in die Flöte hineinsah — oh! was gab es da alles zu sehen! Da war eine Landschaft darin, klein, aber voll Leben: Eine Thoma-sche Landschaft mit Böcklinschen Wolken und Leistikowschen Seen. Rezniceksche Dämchen rümpften die Nasen über Zillesche Gestal-ten, und eine Bauerndirne Meuniers trug einen Arm voll Blumen Or-liks — kurz, die ganze modern Richtung war in der Flöte. Und was machte der Kaiser damit? Er pfiff drauf.

A Fable

There once was an emperor who ruled over an immeasurably large, rich, and beautiful country. And, like any other emperor, he also had a treasure room which in addition to all the sparkling jewels contained a snuffbox. But it was a strange kind of snuffbox. What remarkable things were depicted on its lid! There was a landscape, small but full of life: a Thoma landscape with Böcklin clouds and Leistikow lakes. Reznicek-like ladies turned up their noses at Zille figures, and a peasant maid *à la* Meunier carried an armful of Orlik flowers — in short, the whole artistic *avant-garde* was on this snuff-box. And what do you suppose the emperor did with it? He sneezed at it.

The translation of satire with its highly charged language and frequent verbal play is often a matter of giving full value and compensating for an occasional inability to do so by inserting English locutions that are not in the original but may be deemed to be in the spirit of the satirist. A case in point is another prose piece by Tucholsky; note the title and the last sentence.

Der fromme Angler

Bei Ascona im Tessinischen lebt ein Mann, der hat es mit der
Frömmigkeit und liebt die Lebewesen und alles, was da kreucht
und fleucht. Gut. Nun angelt der Mann aber sehr gern. Und da sitzt
er denn so manchmal am Lago Maggiore und läßt die Beine
baumeln, hält die Angelrute fest und sieht ins Wasser. Und dabei
betet er.
Er betet nämlich: es möge kein Fisch anbeißen.
Weil sich doch Fische immer so quälen müssen, wenn sie am Angel-
haken zappeln, und das möchte der Mann nicht, und da sendet er
denn ein heißes Gebet nach dem andern zum lieben Gott, Abteilung
Lago-Maggiore-Fische: es solle auch gewiß keiner bei ihm anbeis-
sen. Und dann angelt er weiter.
O meine Lieben! Ist dieser Mann nicht so recht eine Allegorie, ja,
ein Symbol? Das ist er. Dieser Mann muß entweder ein alter Jude
sein, oder, verschärfter Fall des Judentums, er ist bei den Jesuiten in
die Lehre gegangen. Er hat das Höchste erreicht, was Menschen erreichen können: er hat die himmlischen Ideale mit seinen sündigen
Trieben zu vereinen gewusst, und das will gekonnt sein. Den Fischen, die da bei ihm zappeln, wird das ja gleich sein; aber ihm ist
es nicht gleich, denn er hat nun beides: die Fische und die Seelen-
ruhe.
Schluß, allgemeiner Ausblick:
Da sitzen sie am Ufer des Lebens . . . oder am Meere des Lebens,
das ist eigentlich noch schöner. . . . Da sitzen sie am Meere des
Lebens und baumeln mit den Beinen und halten die Angelrute ins
Wasser, um den Erfolg zu fischen. Aber wenn sie schlau sind, dann
beten sie dazu und sind: fromme Huren; soziale Bankdirektoren;
demokratische Militärs und privatest die Wahrheit liebende Jour-
nalisten. Sie angeln und sie beten.

Angler, Compleat with Piety

There's a man near Ascona, Switzerland, who's got religion and
loves all living things, all creatures great and small. Well and good.
But the man happens to like fishing. So he sometimes sits by Lake
Maggiore, swinging his legs, holding his fishing rod and looking
into the water. And as he does so, he prays. He prays that no fish
should bite.
You see, the fish are being tortured when they squirm on the hook,
and the man wouldn't want that. So he sends one fervent prayer

after another to the Good Lord, Lake Maggiore Fish Division, to
keep the fish from taking his bait. And then he goes on angling.
My dear readers! Isn't this man a typical allegory, a symbol even?
Tha's what he is. That man must be an old Jew, or — an extreme
case of Jewishness — he must have had Jesuit training. He has at-
tained the highest level that a man can reach: he has learned how to
reconcile heavenly ideals with his sinful drives — and that requires
real skill. It may not make any difference to the fish wriggling on
his hook, but to him it does make a difference, for now he has both:
the fish and peace of mind.
  Conclusion and general application:
there they sit by the bank of life — or by the sea of life, that's really
much better — there they sit by the seal of life, swinging their legs
and dangling their lines into the water in order to hook success. But
if they're shrewd, they pray at the same time, which makes them:
whores who've got religion; civic-minded bank directors;
democratic militarists; and journalists who oh-so-privately love
truth. They prey and they pray.[15]

One of the difficulties in rendering Karl Kraus's wartime satire
"Die Nebensache" (1915), like so many others based on a newspaper item, is the multiple meaning of the word *Lager*, which can
mean "inventory" or "stock" as well as "bed." The solution I found
involves a locution commonly used in Britain (and possibly elsewhere as well) in place of "silent partner," which enjoys greater
currency in North America. The dual sense intended by Kraus is
reproduced if the primary stress is on the first syllable of the first
word.

Die Nebensache

Ich such einen Schwiegervater
der sich mit mir in Konfektion
etabliert; bin 33 Jahre alt, be-
kannt als Reisender und Kon-
fektionär. Verm. verb. J.C.
3378 Exp. d. Bl. Berlin SW.

Cherchez la femme, kann man da wohl nicht mehr sagen. Suchs
Frauerl! Wo ist sie? Er sagt nicht: Einheirat, denn auch der
Schwiegervater ist noch nicht etabliert. Sonst sagten sie wenigstens,

daß sie das Geschäft finden wollen und darum die Frau suchen. Sie brauchten doch einen lebendigen Vorwand. Das fällt jetzt weg; der Schwiegervater ist das Rudiment einer überwundenen Entwicklung, die noch Sentimentalitäten kannte und die Frau beim Warenbestand berücksichtigte. Das ist vorbei. Ein Schwiegervater wird gesucht. Die Tochter kann tot sein, wenn sie will; ist sie bei der Hochzeit da, gut, nicht — nicht. Wird er das Konfektionslager mit dem Schwiegervater teilen! Es ist eine Neuerung in der Damenkonfektionsbranche. Konfektion ohne Dame. Der Glanz antiker Größe durchleuchtet unsere Zeit. Wo ist sie, die dieses Schicksal treffen wird? Die vielleicht die Annonce liest und nicht weiß, daß letzten Endes doch sie gemeint ist! Wo lebt die Konfektionsware? Wo lebt dieses fertige Kleidungsstück von Weib? Wo ist sie, daß ich sie beschwöre, sich jetzt zu verbergen und sich lieber zu töten als der Kadaver dieser Hyäne zu sein. Männer sterben jetzt durch Zufall, Frauen werden gebären, weil zwei sich etablieren wollen. Ein heroisches Zeitalter bricht ein. Beklaget nicht was gewesen. Komm o Morgenrot! Zwei Haderlumpen werden sich in dieser großen Zeit über dem toten Leben eines Mädchens die Hand reichen.

A Minor Detail

> WANTED: A Father-in-Law to go into
> the women's wear business with me.
> Am 33 years old and well known as
> a women's wear salesman and dealer.
> No matchmakers. J.C., Box 3378, c/o
> this newspaper, Berlin S.W.

I suppose "Cherchez la femme" no longer applies here. Go find mama, boy! Where is she? He doesn't speak of marrying into the business, because the father-in-law himself isn't in business yet. Normally such people at least said they wanted to find a business and were therefore looking for a wife. After all, they needed a living pretext. This is now eliminated; the father-in-law is the vestige of an obsolete stage of development which still had sentimentality and included a wife in the inventory. That's over with. Wanted: a father-in-law. The daughter can be dead if she likes. If she is present at the wedding, fine; if not, that's all right too. He'll just take the father-in-law as his sleeping partner. This is an innovation in women's wear: wear without women. The glow of classical greatness suffuses our time. Where is the woman whom such a fate will befall, who will perhaps read this ad without knowing that in the final analysis it concerns her? Where does the women's wear live? Where does this ready-made apparel of a woman live? Where is she, that I may implore her to go into hiding and kill herself sooner than become the cadaver of this hyena? Men are now dying accidental deaths; women will give birth because two men want to go into business. A heroic age is dawning. Do not mourn what has been. Come, O dawn! Two scoundrels will in these great times shake hands over the dead life of a girl.

At the risk of sounding anticlimactic or repetitive, I should like to close by restating what I have come to consider as the foremost commandments for a translator of satire: Keep faith with the satirist; join him (if need be, across continents and ages) as an equal partner in the forging of an effective weapon made of language; be, so to speak, on the same wavelength; be scrupulously attentive to the satirist's methods and purposes. Since these methods and purposes are not always properly understood or appreciated, the translator of satire will often share in the incomprehension, opprobrium, and even downright hostility that tend to be a satirist's lot. But the satisfaction of an uncommonly challenging job well done will almost invariably outweigh any such risks.

NOTES

1. C.E. Vulliamy, ed. *The Anatomy of Satire*. London: Michael Joseph, 1950, p. 10.

2. Edgar Johnson, ed. *A Treasury of Satire*. New York: Simon & Schuster, 1945, p. 34, 36.

3. E. Pawel, "A Voice Before the Silence." *Commentary* LVII, 12, Dec. 1968, p. 106.

4. *In These Great Times: A Karl Kraus Reader*, ed. by H. Zohn. Montreal: Engendra Press, 1976, p. 259.

5. M. Eastman, *Enjoyment of Laughter*. New York: Simon & Schuster, 1936, p. 229.

6. E. Heller, "Karl Kraus," in *The Disinherited Mind*. New York: Farra, Straus &

Cadahy, 1957, p. 239.

7. K. Kraus, *Half-Truths and One-and-a-Half Truths*. Montreal: Engendra, 1976, p. 67.

8. Cleveland: World Publishing Co., p. 413.

9. London: Weidenfeld & Nicolson, p. 11.

10. T. Szasz, *Karl Kraus and the Soul Doctors*. Baton Rouge: Louisiana State University Press, 1976, p. 103.

11. Cf. my polemic with Dr. Szasz and his editor in *ATA Chronicle*, Jan.-Feb. 1977 (pp. 7-9) and Apr.-May 1977 (pp. 2-6).

12. A. Appelfeld, *Badenheim 1939*. Boston: David R. Godine, 1980, p. 80.

13. W. Toman, *A Kindly Contagion*. New York: Bobbs Merrill Co., 1959.

14. P. Bridgewater, ed. *Let's Face It: Poems by Erich Kästner*. London: Jonathan Cape 1963, p. 113. H. Zohn, "Translations from Erich Kästner." *Aufbau* (N.Y.), Feb. 10, 1959, p. 32.

15. For another (and, to my mind, weaker) translation, see Bryan P. Grenville, *Kurt Tucholsky: The Ironic Sentimentalist*. London: Oswald Wolff, 1980, pp. 117-8.

Translating and Transplanting
the Viennese Cabaret

A Workshop on Helmut Qualtinger's
Wien wird wieder Weltstadt

Harry Zohn and Gerald Chapple
Brandeis U/McMaster U

What justification is there for transplanting to frequently alien or barren soil flowers of "jest, satire, irony, and deeper significance," to use a phrase made a "wingèd word" by the German playwright Christian Dietrich Grabbe? Surely the motivation of a translator who undertakes the arduous and thankless task of expressing the wit and wisdom of a foreign writer whose stock in trade is essentially ethnic humor couched in the vernacular or dialect of that writer's language is precisely what motivates a good journalist, teacher, or raconteur telling a funny story: an eagerness to share with a wider audience what may be expected to convey insight and cheer. But how can the patois or dialect of one language be rendered into another? This is a problem that will have as many solutions (or non-solutions) as there are intrepid translators willing to attempt the nearly impossible.

A score of "intrepid translators" held a workshop at the colloquium to try their hands, tongues, and minds at solving the problem in several of its ramifications. The leader, Harry Zohn, served up a text from a challenging genre—the Viennese cabaret. *Wien wird wieder Weltstadt* was published in 1975 in Helmut Qualtinger's *Der Mörder und andere Leut'* (Munich: Langen-Müller, pp. 91-96). Qualtinger, with Carl Merz and Gerhard Bronner, formed the satirical triumvirate that presided over the golden age of the Viennese postwar cabaret in the 1950s and 1960s. Widely admired at home, they have until recently escaped translation—undoubtedly because most of their work is in the Viennese dialect and also because, like Vienna's potent new wine, the characteristic local types do not travel well. We will discuss below a recent attempt at giving Qualtinger a British passport; but there are some questions of principle and method that should be raised at the outset. Do you substitute one world capital for another? Then what happens to local terms and references? Can we replace one major urban dialect with another? And how to handle nuances of social language levels? Since the text belongs to the performing arts, how do you make it playable? What about questions of dated language for an audience of the 1980s or 1990s? Many answers to these thorny questions have of course been proposed before now, and since they apply to related genres as well, a brief look at the experience of a master translator of musicals into German might be in order before we return to the case at hand.

Between two languages there are dainty, fragile bridges across an abyss of misunderstanding. When two languages meet, they often walk past each other mutely, or worse, they talk past each other." These words are from the pen of Robert Gilbert, a Berlin-born writer and translator of song lyrics as well as a poet, and they may be found in the Afterword to his German version of *My Fair Lady*, one of twenty musicals Gilbert adapted for the German-speaking stage. Gilbert speaks of a mediator between two entirely different word-worlds and heterogeneous mentalities, an adventurous *Grenzgänger* (a person who crosses a border, especially one who does so illegally) commonly called translator: "On his left, a flaming postulate: faithfulness to the original. On his right, loyalty to his clansmen. To do justice to both, he constantly swings back and forth like a pendulum. He could also be compared to a tightrope walker performing his breakneck balancing act on a thin thread of synonyms, juggling seventeen dictionaries on the tip of his nose, though only for aesthetic reasons; he rarely opens them, for he never, or hardly ever, finds in them what he is so desperately looking for." Translation, then, is nothing but an echo, and a translator's greatest reward comes when this echo is so little perceived that it seems to be "not a shout from afar, but the familiar voice of someone talking in the next room."

A few samples from *My Fair Lady* (so titled in the translation as well) may be in order here. Gilbert decided that the closest German equivalent of Cockney dialect was the tough and flavorsome speech of Berlin. This does not mean that the Ascot Gavotte was performed at the legendary Grunewald wood auction or another kind of Spree spree, but Gilbert did enliven the British scene by having that famous flower girl struggle with standard German. Eliza's language had to be pruned of Berlinisms that involve the modification of certain vowels, consonants, and diphthongs and lead to slurred and sloppy speech. Since Berliners have trouble with umlauts, turning *ü* sounds into *ee* sounds, the progression in the celebrated "Rain in Spain" number is from the dialectal "Es jrient so jrien, wenn Spaniens Blieten blieh'n" (meaning that things get pretty green when Spain's blossoms bloom) to the triumphantly High German "Es grünt so grün, wenn Spaniens Blüten blüh'n." That elocution lesson involving all those aspirated places where hurricanes hardly happen comes out as "Ich se-he Krä-hen in der Nä-he . . . Re-he se-he ich e-her nä-her" (I see crows nearby; deer I see at even closer range). While Doolittle does remain a dustman (in North American terms, a trash collector or garbageman), his "With a little bit of luck" is Berlinized into "Mit 'nem kleenen Stückchen Glück," and his daughter's "Wouldn't it be loverly?" is accurately rendered as "Wäre das nich wundaschön?" But despite Gilbert's skill, the basic illogic remains: Eliza Doolittle, her mentor Henry Higgins, and the others clearly live in London, but the wit and wisdom of those speaking cockney English is presented as Berlinese—an uneasy alliance between London and Berlin.

Returning to Qualtinger, we find a recent translation has produced an even more unholy misalliance between London and Vienna. *Herr Karl*, the long and maudlin monologue of a mordantly-drawn, instantly-recognizable Viennese type, an unprincipled, outwardly *gemütlich* but really ruthless member of the lower or lower middle classes, has been Englished and anglicized into the phenomenon of a "Cockney Karl." In Adolf Opel's *Anthology of Modern Austrian Literature* (London: Oswald Wolff, 1981, pp. 171-75), Peter Hutchinson presents some of the self-exculpatory musings of a man who seems to be living not in "Vyenner" on the "Danyewb Canal" but in a workingman's district of London. References to such "Orstrian" places as Laaerberg and the "Ring an' the 'eldenplatz" cannot overcome the "pub" and the "porridge." One gets the impression that "Mister Karl" is not a "ruddy furriner" from Vienna who once admired "'itler" but an authentic Londoner. What can posters with "mottoes from Goethe" possibly mean to a man whose Briticisms like "scarper" and "shipin' our ends" are bound to puzzle readers in most parts of the English world? It may, of course, be that just as Gilbert deemed a "Berliner Pflanze" to be the best equivalent of Eliza Doolittle, Hutchinson discerned the cockney in Herr Karl (which, in any case, is a dubious compliment to the former, unless one believes that "little people" are alike no matter where they live).

It is probably true that Americans have a higher tolerance for Briticisms than the British do for Americanisms (or even American spelling), but there is a limit that should not be exceeded. A few items from a book published and printed in the United States not so long ago (*Last Waltz in Vienna* by George Clare, a Viennese-born Britisher; New York: Holt, Rinehart & Winston, 1982) will exemplify this. There are references to a grammar school (high school), its forms and form masters (homeroom teachers), a doctor's surgery (office), a girl's knickers (underpants), trams (streetcars), a box-room (storage closet), and a tuck-shop (snack shop or refreshment stand). Even though Americans don't mind an occasional lorry running on petrol and know that Britishers like to read a good leader in a newspaper, a number of the above terms are bound to mislead them, if they are understood at all. Witness, too, the confusion caused by Tom Stoppard's recent translation of Johann Nestroy's rambunctious Viennese *Einen Jux will er sich machen* as the ever-so British *On the Razzle*. Even in "English"-speaking Canada, radio advertisements were forced to add deciphering footnotes after announcing the title—the nearest verbal clue, "razzle-dazzle," provided no help. Why not a title like *On the Town*, or *Painting the Town Red*? These could transplant the Viennese playwright into North American theaters more gracefully and intelligibly. Maybe the best way out of these dilemmas is to translate into a kind of general, universal, or neutral English.

This was the course chosen by the workshop. Although the translators' origin or vantage point is not left in doubt (in this instance, they all live in Canada or the United States), they decided not to substitute one metropolitan dialect for another. The basic paradoxical hybridization of any translation (see the above remarks on *My Fair Lady*) was minimized: local references were retained— there was no transmogrification of Rimini into Miami Beach, or St. Pölten into Hoboken or St. Louis. These changes might have been called for if we had chosen to emulate Marc Blitzstein, who avoided the clash of world capitals by shifting his adaptation of the Brecht-Weill *Dreigroschenoper* to New York in the 1870s. But we felt that a foreign locale would create more problems than it would solve, so that the need to ponder over an ungainly Americanism like "hot dog" for "Burenwurst" was eliminated in advance.

Apart from the geographical question, Blitzstein's shift to another century raises a further relevant point: dating the translation, and avoiding any anachronisms that could result. Our overriding concern was that the text be playable to-day, a generation after its composition. The dialogue takes its life from the everyday spoken word; this demanded that equal attention be paid to the accuracy of expression and the need for immediate comprehension by the audience or else the bubbly wit goes flat and the sketch moves too slowly to come to life.

A further bedeviling communication problem was to differentiate the speech levels that are part and parcel of the characterization. The vendor, who is clearly from a different background, begins by speaking High German, then he intersperses it with Viennese. Now since all social classes speak this marvellous dialect, we were faced with an untranslatable nuance. The only approximation was for us to switch from more formal to increasingly colloquial English as the *rapprochement* of the two characters gained momentum until the commercially intimate climax was reached. Naturally, many subtleties of tone, voice, and gesture are missing in print (in both texts, for that matter), but we all should bear in mind that actors are to act and speak, and an audience is to laugh. What is the purpose of the text if not to function as a supple springboard for the reader's imagination—that silent auditor who has to hear the words inwardly and envisage their delivery before a live and lively audience? Behind our striving for a *playable* translation lie the modest aims of promoting its performance and of stimulating much-needed translations of other works by the most compelling Viennese satirist of our time.

The annotated translation offered below is not meant to smack of the well-thumbed dictionary or the scholarly study. It is, among other things, a document reflecting the productive and animated quality of the collective enterprise that spawned it. In preparing the final version for publication we have recorded several alternative renderings sparked by the debates that arose from the truly convivial, "colloquial" atmosphere. Some of the more ribald *obiter dicta* successfully resisted being cut; their levity is intended to convey to the regrettably absent, collaborating reader something of the spirit of scholarly fun that infused the session and blended most appropriately with the genius of our typically witty and worldly cabaret sketch. Here the authors wish to thank all those who worked over the text in the workshop session, with a special bow to two graduate students from the University of Toronto, Rick Sikora and Walter Hartmann, for their extra help. May the text and its annotations be just as entertaining and instructive for the reader as the delightful task of creating them was for us.

Wien wird wieder Weltstadt[1]

(*Ein Burenwurststand.*[2] *Davor eine ältere*[3] *Prostituierte und ein Blumenverkäufer.*)

Prostituierte: Jetzt regnets erst recht.

Blumenverkäufer: Für meine Blumen zu spät.

Prostituierte: Zwei Kunden hab i ghabt, und morgen wollt ichs zusperren.[4]

Blumenverkäufer: Wann haben Sie zuletzt Urlaub gemacht?

Prostituierte: I darf gar net dran denken . . . Rimini . . .

Blumenverkäufer: Dort regnets auch. Manchmal.

Prostituierte: Schmeckt Ihnen die Burenwurst?

Blumenverkäufer: Nach Regen.

Prostituierte: Kein Mensch auf der Straßn.

Blumenverkäufer: Warum gehens net z' Haus?[5]

---

1. "Metropolis" would denote the size of the city but not the nuance of classiness needed to act as a foil for the two "worldly" speakers. The catchy alliteration of the title has been reduced; the option is still there if the actors choose to play the piece with an accent. In that case the title could be spoken, "Vienna — A Vorld-Class City Vunce Again". The verb in the title was dropped to enhance the rhythm and brevity.

2. This type of sausage – little-known elsewhere – is almost at the horsemeat level, but the neutral term "sausage" says enough to the English-speaking audience. "Hot-dog stand" is of course too specifically American. Cf. note E 35 below.

3. Elderly" goes too far in the direction of respectfulness. "Middle-aged" is possible, but we opted for "aging," which concisely communicates that the bloom is off this particular rose.

4. Several people felt that, given the risqué subject matter and bawdy tone of the piece, Qualtinger might have meant a *double entendre* here. If so, "lock it up" might be an alternative translation.

5. The vendor now congenially shifts into Viennese. We could find only a rough equivalent by transcribing the sounds of his colloquial language as he puts himself closer to her level.

Vienna — A World-Class City Once Again

(*A sausage stand. In front of it, an aging prostitute and a flower vendor.*)

Prostitute: Now it's really coming down.

Vendor: Too late for my flowers.

Prostitute: I had two customers[6] and to-morrow I was gonna close up shop.

Vendor: When did you last take a vacation?

Prostitute: Don' even wanna think about it . . . Rimini[7] . . .

Vendor: Rains there too.[8] Sometimes.

Prostitute: How's the sausage taste?

Vendor: Like rain.

Prostitute: Not a soul out here on the street.

Vendor: Why doncha g'wan home?

---

6. "Clients" would be just as acceptable here because it is on the same "respectable" linguistic level. We reserved the colloquial and lower-level translations for "Kunden," "tricks" and "johns" until later when the two people are on friendlier terms.

7. San Tropez was offered as a better-kown Mediterranean beach resort, but it was felt to be too classy for the lady in question.

8. There is an opportunity for an English pun here which Qualtinger of course did not have: "You can get soaked there too."

Prostituierte: Einen muß ich heut noch kriegen.

Blumenverkäufer: I kann meine Rosen auf den Mist haun.

Prostituierte: Wie kommen mir dazu?[9]

Blumenverkäufer: Was meinens?

Prostituierte: Na, daß wir so ohne Gewerkschaft . . . Ohne Schutz
. . .

Blumenverkäufer: Ich weiß, wen ich wähl.

Prostituierte: Meine Herren werden immer blöder. Heut war einer
aus St. Pölten da.

Blumenverkäufer: Dort gibts doch ein'n Puff.

Prostituierte: Dort san zu viel Leut . . . Und man kennt ihn . . . Er
is in der Handelskammer . . . Lang hat er mir erzählt von seinem
Beruf.[10]

Blumenverkäufer: Wie Sie das aushalten. Das viele Reden.

Prostituierte: I merk mirs ja nicht.[11] Ausländer[12] kommen so wenig. Das san Festwochen. Blumen . . . Einer hat mir Eins-A-Rosen
kauft Dann is er mir nachgangen von Lokal zu Lokal[13] und hat sich
beschwert, daß schon welk san . . . Bei Ihnere Händ' wird die
schönste Blume welk, hab i gsagt . . . Sie können sich nicht vorstel-
len, was ich für Beschwerden zu hörn krieg. Gut, manchmal komm
ich nicht zum Waschen oder zum Schminken. Aber die könnten ja
warten. Sofort wollen sies immer.

---

9. Some good alternative suggestions: "How'd we wind up like this?" "Why'd
this have ta happen ta us?" "How'd we get into this fix?" We chose the briefest
rendering.

10. The German word clearly shows that this was a respected member of society,
but "profession" sounded stilted in English. Although "job" or "business" was
possible, we compromised on the more neutral "work."

11. Since it is part of the lady's role to spend much of her time listening, this
line produced several sympathetic suggestions. "It goes in one ear and out the
other," and "It rolls right off me" were accurate but rather long. Once "Who
remembers?" was tried, the syntactic pattern prompted the final choice. "So who
listens?" just barely lost out because of its Yiddish overtones.

12. "Tourists" was rejected because it could include Austrian visitors to the
Vienna Festival as well.

13. "Pub," "dive," and "joint" were felt to be less international than "bar."

Prostitute: Gotta turn one more trick to-day.

Vendor: Guess I'll have ta chuck my roses.

Prostitute: Where'd we go wrong?

Vendor: Whad'ya mean?

Prostitute: Well, us with no union . . . no protection . . .

Vendor: I know who I'm voting for.

Prostitute: My gentlemen are getting dumber and dumber. To-day I had one from St. Pölten.

Vendor: Don't they have a cat-house[14] there?

Prostitute: Too many people there . . . and they know him . . . He's in the Chamber of Commerce . . . He went on and on about his work.

Vendor: How can you stand it! All that talk.

Prostitute: Who listens? I hardly get any foreigners. Some Vienna Festival! Flowers . . . A guy bought me real classy[15] roses. Then he followed me from bar to bar 'n' complained they were already wiltin' . . . With paws like you got, the nicest flowers are gonna wilt, sez I . . . You can't imagine the bitchin' I get to hear. O.K., so I don't always wash or put on my face. As if they couldn't wait. But they gotta have it right away.[16]

---

14. This is even more colloquial than "whorehouse" and is on the same plane with "Puff" – reason enough to reject the more formal "brothel" or the euphemistic "house of ill repute."

15. There were numerous contestants here: "A-Number One," "Grade A," "long-stem," "first-class." The phrase selected has the advantage of ironically echoing the translated title

16. The lady's more excited and colloquial narration of her anecdote requires a similar freedom in the English translation.

Blumenverkäufer: Keine Erotiker.[17]

Prostituierte: Bei die Kongresse kommt manchmal einer.

Blumenverkäufer: Mich laßt oft mein Gärtner im Stich.

Prostituierte: Warum tun wir das alles.

Blumenverkäufer: Weil wir in unserm Wien bleiben wollen. Aus welchem Bezirk[18] sind Sie?

Prostituierte: Essling . . . I weiß gar net, was für ein Bezirk das is.

Blumenverkäufer: Ich bin von Währing.

Prostituierte: Schmeckt Ihnen die Burenwurst?

Blumenverkäufer: Seitdem ich weiß, was die da einehaun.

Prostituierte: So arg is das?

Blumenverkäufer: Sehr arg. I geh heut nirgends mehr hin.

Prostituierte: I wahrscheinlich a net. Übermorgen hab i Untersuchung.[19]

Blumenverkäufer: Das könnt i net jeden Monat . . .

Prostituierte: Das is sehr unangenehm.[20] Scheußlich is. Ärger als der ärgste Klient.

Blumenverkäufer: I steh so blöd da mit meine Blumen. Wollns eine?

Prostituierte: Bei dem Regen? (Nimmt zögernd die Blume.) Die tun mir ja leid.

---

17. A challenge. The German word is at once more delicate and witty; our neologism could retain only the humour. "No lovers with class" was accurate but rather flat.

18. "District" would be proper, but it is ambiguous in English. Unlike Währing, Essling is not a district but a town out in the sticks, which explains her answer. There was no way to convey this nuance to a foreign audience so the colloquial phrase, "part of town," seemed to fit the context best.

19. The routine, regular examination the city officials.

20. "Unpleasant" is too genteel, whereas "pain" works on two levels, the physical and the slangy one.

Vendor: No sexperts.

Prostitute: Guys on conventions sometimes.

Vendor: Sometimes my supplier lets me down.

Prostitute: Why are we doing all this?

Vendor: Because we wanna stay in our dear old Vienna. What part of town are you from?

Prostitute: Essling . . . I don' even know what part that is.

Vendor: I'm from Währing myself.

Prostitute: How's the sausage?

Vendor: Since I found out what all they put in it . . .[21]

Prostitute: It's that bad?

Vendor: Pretty bad. I ain't goin' nowhere else tonight.

Prostitute: Me neither, probably. Day after to-morrow I gotta go for my monthly check-up.

Vendor: I couldn't stand goin' every month to . . .

Prostitute: It's a real pain. Horrible. Worse than the kinkiest customer.[22].

Vendor: I feel like an idiot standin' aroun' with my flowers. Want one?

Prostitute: In this rain? (*Hesitates, then takes the flower.*) I really feel sorry for them.

---

21. Although this may sound weak for "einehaun," "what they shove into it" or "stick into it" struck us as being too drastic in English.

22. "Customer" by itself, for "Kunde," would be rather bland (cf. note 6 above), but the qualifying adjective gives her words the right semantic nuance. The alliteration tries to carry over the repeated "ärger . . . ärgste." "Worse than the worst kind of customer," or "Worse than the weirdest customer," would perhaps be more accurate and would retain the alliteration; but these sounded a little flat next to the contemporary "kinkiest."

Blumenverkäufer: Sie haben ein gutes Herz.[23]

Prostituierte: Drum bin i ja so weit kommen.[24] Erst kommt einer, da machts Spaß, dann kommt der Nächste, da wirds erst richtig. Beim Achten oder Zwölften weiß man, was man will, und wenn man an die Zwanzig is, sagen schon manche Hur. Manchmal auch: liebe Hur . . . Oder: Frau Hur . . .

Blumenverkäufer: Sind Sie manchmal auch leidenschaftlich?

Prostituierte: Wanns richtig lauft und der Herr entsprechend jung is. Amal in der Zeit.

Blumenverkäufer: Und ältere? Können doch auch zärtlich[25] sein.

Prostituierte: Was die oft machen, das kann ich Ihnen gar nicht erzählen.

Blumenverkäufer: Nichts Menschliches ist mir fremd.[26] Habens amal einen Neger ghabt?

Prostituierte: Ja, öfter.

Blumenverkäufer: Stimmt das, was man so sagt?

Prostituierte: Na, schwarz sans net unten, wenns das meinen. Unter der Vorhaut san alle gleich.[27]

Blumenverkäufer: Interessant. Und die Chinesen?

Prostituierte: Die lachen immer dabei.

---

23. Because it was a little too free, we resisted the temptation to refer to the proverbial "prostitute with a heart of gold" here, in spite of her "bargain rate" at the end.

24. "That's how I got this far" was a second choice; both translations carry over her unconscious irony.

25. "Romantic" was chosen over "gentle" or "loving" because it sets up her unwittingly undercutting reply to the vendor's indirect approach – for that is what the line amounts to, as we see later.

26. Concealing his disappointment under a classical tag, the vendor reveals that he is not without traces of urbanity and a good education. He elegantly recovers and tries a different tack.

27. To retain the two inversions of subject and verb would make her language sound too formal and elevated for her character.

Vendor: You've got a kind heart.

Prostitute: That's how I got where I am. You get one guy an' it's fun, then the next one comes along an' you really get into it. When you get to number eight or twelve, you know what you want, an' when you get to twenty, a lot o' them start to say "whore" to me. Sometimes: "Dear whore" . . . Or "Madam Whore" . . .

Vendor: Do you get turned on[28] sometimes?

Prostitute: When things go right an' the guy's young enough. Oncet in a blue moon.[29]

Vendor: And what about older men? Now really, can't they be romantic too?

Prostitute: I couldn't begin to tell ya what *they* often do!

Vendor: Nothing human is alien to me. Didja ever have a black man?

Prostitute: Yeah, lots o' times.

Vendor: Is it true what they say about them?

Prostitute: Well, they ain't black down *there,* if that's whatcha mean. They're all the same under the foreskin.

Vendor: Interesting. And what about Chinese?

Prostitute: They always smile[30] when they're doin' it.

---

28. The contemporary slang expression was so apt for the context that it won out over the accurate alternatives, "excited," "passionate," and "really involved."

29. "Oncet" renders the Viennese "Amal." The English idiom suggested itself because of the film from the 1950s, *The Moon is Blue,* which some in the audience might remember as being sexually daring for its day.

30. "Laugh," or even the freer "giggle," would be quire acceptable here. Instead, we capitalized on the less emotive, but powerful, enigmatic Oriental "smile."

Blumenverkäufer: Darf ich Sie noch zu einer Burenwurst . . . Oder wollns a Debreziner?

Prostituierte: Na, na,[31] meine Linie, die halt ich mir. Gegens Alter kann man nix machen. Aber bei der Figur bin i stur.[32] I fürcht mi oft.

Blumenverkäufer: Was denn?

Prostituierte: Daß einer amal alte Hur zu mir sagt.

Blumenverkäufer: Aber bei Ihrer Erscheinung. Die Haar . . . Der Blick . . .

Prostituierte: Hörens auf, wir san ja Kollegen.[33] Wie heißen Sie?

Blumenverkäufer: Znirsch.

Prostituierte: Sie müssen[34] doch einen Vornam –

Blumenverkäufer: Herr Znirsch.

(*Geräusche der Rettung.*)

Prostituierte: Schon wieder ein lieber Herr Toter.

Blumenverkäufer (lachend): Sie spinnen ja.

Prostituierte: Vorige Wochn habens a Kollegin von mir erwürgt .

---

31. A contender heremost suitable for the stage – was the negative, non-verbal "Uh-uh."

32. After several attempts at a literal translation were made, Harry Zohn took the honors by hitting upon a way to retain the rhyme.

33. "Colleague," in English, would sound out of place for the prostitute (cf. also G 116: Kollegin), who recognizes that they both are in the same game of selling something. They are not in *exactly* the same game, so the colloquial phrase selected was preferable to "same business" or "racket." This time, she has caught the vendor's more direct approach, rejecting it, yet re- sponding enough to ask the first, obvious, personal question. And his refusal to answer her in the expected way keeps the ambiguous tone of formality and hoped-for intimacy that suits the game they are playing.

34. Simple words can be tricky. Here, as elsewhere, the more colloquial "got to" was preferable to "must" or "need to." Cf. p. 218: notwendig, and p. 219, five ll. up.

Vendor: May I treat you to another knockwurst . . . Or maybe you'd like a bratwurst?[35]

Prostitute: No thanks, gotta watch my waistline. Can't keep from gettin' old. But I won't let my figger get any bigger. I get so scared sometimes.

Vendor: Scared o' what?

Prostitute: That a guy's gonna call me "old whore" some day.

Vendor: But with your looks . . . that hair . . . those eyes . . .

Prostitute: Oh, cut it out, we're in the same game, ain't we? What's your name?

Vendor: Znirsch.

Prostitute: But you gotta have a Christian . . . (*An ambulance siren sounds.*)

Prostitute: Another Mr. Deadman.[36]

Vendor (*laughs*): You're off your rocker.

Prostitute: Last week someone strangled one of us girls . . .

---

35. The English-speaking audience is more likely to know the sausages substituted here on the menu than the two named in the original. The vendor's recommendation of a better-quality Debreziner shows that he is preparing to close in.

36. A puzzle. Freer alternatives were "Dear Mr. Corpse" (too awkward and bumpy), "Another Mr. Nice Guy dead and gone" (too long and fussy), and "Another poor dead sucker" (a close second because of its idiomatic flavor).

. . . Keine Spur vom Täter. Nasenpeter[37] haben wir zu ihr gsagt. So a Nasn, und tot.

Blumenverkäufer: Gehn wir z'Haus.

Prostituierte: Seitdems den Strich[38] verlegt haben, is überhaupt nix los.

Blumenverkäufer: An Kunden wüßt i noch.

Prostituierte: Wen?

Blumenverkäufer (*zeigt auf sich*): Mich.

Prostituierte: Herr Znirsch, das is wirklich net notwendig.

Blumenverkäufer: Habens Angst vor mir?

Prostituierte: Mir kennen sich[39] schon so lang.

Blumenverkäufer: Na? Und das ist unsere Zeit. Aber anstrengen müssens Ihnen schon.[40]

---

37. The Viennese term ("Nasenpäuli" is also heard) called for a free English equivalent. Fortunately, "schnozz" suits the context – few would sense its Yiddish origin here – and those who remember Jimmy Durante would catch the reference to his nickname. If this sounds too dated, then "Pinnocchio" stands in the wings.

38. The German word succinctly says it all, but English has no equivalent. "Red-light district" suggests appropriate establishments but the ladies here are out on the street (the wisecrack that they might have red "tail"-lights was laughed out of court). "Beat" or "territory" were approximations, but the contemporary "turf" would be best understood to-day, although it would not have been in the 1960s (the same applies to "black man" for "Neger," p. 214 above). Apparently, the city administration had recently moved the ladies to another part of Vienna.

39. Her colloquial Viennese is reflected in the English: the technically more correct "each other" becomes "one another."

40. This gag line is a teaser, and elicited a host of intriguing equivalents for "anstrengen." The English pun latent in "put out," in the twin sense of making a great effort and of performing the required sexual activities, was a strong candidate, but the pun only works if you know the German original, which an English-speaking cabaret audience would not. The word-play with "butt" is somewhat milder but keeps the gag going. Combining the semantic and physiological aspects of "working one's butt off," someone – who shall remain nameless – suggested that Qualtinger, had he been writing in English, might have termed this an "a-popo-plexical" crux. Maybe.

They haven't a clue who did it. We useta call her "Schnozzola."
What a schnozz on her, and now she's dead.

Vendor: Let's g'wan home.

Prostitute: Since they shifted our turf here, there's been no action.[41]

Vendor: Bet I could get you another john.[42]

Prostitute: Who's that?

Vendor (*points to himself*): Me.

Prostitute: Mister Znirsch, you really don't have ta.

Vendor: Scared o' me?

Prostitute: We've known one another such a long time.

Vendor: So?[43] An' now it's time for us. But cher gonna have ta
work your butt off.

---

41. The contemporary phrase has appropriate "business" connotations (including a "piece of the action"), which is why it was given the nod over "nothin'
doin'" and "not a damn thing goin' on."

42. The vendor's use of Viennese called for a colloquial term in English (cf. p.
209, note 6)). This also helps keep his language on her level for his unexpected
revelation at the *dénouement*, when he makes his final move.

43. Or "So what?" – as long as the actor delivers the line with the necessary
accompanying shrug that both translations invite.

Prostituierte: I kanns noch immer net glauben.

Blumenverkäufer (*gibt ihr den Blumenstrauß*): Ich bitte.[44]

Prostituierte: Na gut (*hakt sich ein*): Vielleicht mach ich auch einen Sonderpreis. Ausverkauf.[45] Komm.

Blumenverkäufer (*im Abgehen*): Die Burenwürst müssens Ihnen aber selber zahln . . .

(*Dunkel.*)

---

44. The more literal translations, "If you please," or "Allow me," do not have the same invitational overtones as the English phrase chosen. "Be my guest" also sets up the irony of the last line – and the last word – of the sketch, which owes much of its humour to the reminder that this is still a business deal between two business people.

45. "Clearance sale" or "Reduced to clear" might have served equally well but, even allowing for her hyperbole, they sounded too final for the temporary bargain struck at the happy ending.

Prostitute: I still don't believe it.[46]

Vendor (*hands her his bunch of flowers*): Be my guest.

Prostitute: Well, awright. (*Takes his arm.*) Maybe I'll give you a discount. It's on sale. C'mon, honey.[47]

Vendor: (*as he exits*): But cher gotta pay for your own knockwurst . . .

(*Blackout.*)

---

46. A second choice was the cliché, "But why is all this happening to us?" "Pinch me, I'm dreaming!" is freer but was felt to be too "romantic" even for this context.

47. How to render into English this one time where there is a shift from *Sie* to *du*—a classic problem? A frequent solution is to use the Christian name in English, but *Mr.* Znirsch deliberately kept that to himself. The phrase chosen was felt to be intimate enough for the occasion.